These wise and experience ... *tive discipline is all about e* ... *, ... punishment.* This well-organized and beautifully written book shows parents how they can employ plenty of common sense and a lot of love to teach their children invaluable life lessons that will enable them to become thoughtful, responsible, caring citizens of the world.

—Dr. Michael Meyerhoff, Ed.D., Executive Director, The Education for Parenthood Information Center

This is the most important book you can buy for your family—now and for the future.

—Victoria Moran, author of *Creating a Charmed Life*

The best book I have read to teach appropriate behavior and to encourage kind, resilient, and caring children.

—Nicole Wise, coauthor of *The Over-Scheduled Child: Avoiding the Hyper-Parenting Trap*, and mother of four

By following the suggestions in this simple, easy-to-read book, you are building a foundation of peace, love, empathy, and self-control in your children's lives. You will be forever grateful.

—Wally Amos, author of *The Cookie Never Crumbles: Inspirational Recipes for Everyday Living*

This book should be required reading for any parent who wants to react to preschooler conflicts calmly and nonviolently. This invaluable guide is a treasury of practical principles and concrete strategies for answering the universal childrearing challenges parents face every day.

—Linda Lantieri, coauthor of *Waging Peace in Our Schools,* and Founding Director of the Resolving Conflict Creatively Program of Educators for Social Responsibility

If all parents could follow the path outlined in this book, wars would be reduced to a memory of madness from a long time ago. I'd like to thank the authors for writing a book that helps parents answer the question, "What part can I play in trying to make sure that my children grow up to be confident, productive, happy people with their self-esteem intact?"

—Peter Yarrow, member of Peter, Paul, and Mary, and founder of Operation Respect: Don't Laugh at Me

DISCIPLINE without SHOUTING or SPANKING

**Practical Solutions to the Most Common
Preschool Behavior Problems**

Jerry Wyckoff, Ph.D.
Barbara C. Unell

Meadowbrook Press
Distributed by Simon & Schuster
New York

Library of Congress Cataloging-in-Publication Data
Wyckoff, Jerry, 1935–
    Discipline without shouting or spanking: practical solutions to the
most common preschool behavior problems / Jerry Wyckoff, Barbara C.
Unell.
        p. cm.
    Includes bibliographical references and index.
    ISBN 0-88166-410-3 (Meadowbrook) ISBN 0-7432-2854-5 (Simon &
Schuster)
        1. Discipline of children—Handbooks, manuals, etc I. Unell, Barbara
C., 1951– II. Title.

HQ770.4 .W93 2002
649.64—dc21

                                                          2002020182

Editorial Director: Christine Zuchora-Walske
Editor: Joseph Gredler
Proofreader: Megan McGinnis
Production Manager: Paul Woods
Desktop Publishing: Danielle White, Mark Jacobson
Cover Photo: Tony Garcia, SuperStock
Index: Beverlee Day

© 1984, 2002 by Jerry Wyckoff and Barbara Unell

Published by: Meadowbrook Press
                 5451 Smetana Drive
                 Minnetonka, MN 55343

www.meadowbrookpress.com

BOOK TRADE DISTRIBUTION by Simon & Schuster, a division of
Simon and Schuster, Inc., 1230 Avenue of the Americas, New York, New
York 10020

06   05   10 9 8 7 6 5

Printed in the United States of America

Dedication

This book is dedicated to our adult children,
Christopher Wyckoff, Allison Wyckoff,
Justin Unell, and Amy Unell,
for their unsolicited and priceless
contributions to this book.

Acknowledgments

We would like to thank all the parents and other caregivers who continue to reinforce our belief that disciplining without shouting or spanking will always be the kindest and most effective way to teach children how to become self-sufficient, empathetic, responsible, self-controlled people.

We would also like to thank Bruce Lansky for his continued confidence in this book over the past two decades. Our thoughtful, dedicated editor, Joseph Gredler, has been our able steward during the revision and expansion of *Discipline without Shouting or Spanking*, which has been a reliable and trustworthy road map for hundreds of thousands of parents. We are grateful to Meadowbrook Press for the opportunity to help a new generation of parents discipline their children in loving, practical ways.

Contents

Preface

If you are a parent, recognize that it is the most important calling and rewarding challenge you have. What you do every day, what you say and how you act, will do more to shape the future of America than any other factor.

—Marion Wright Edelman

All children—especially preschoolers—create discipline problems, no matter how "perfect" the children or parents might be. Both well-adjusted and not-so-well-adjusted children of every socioeconomic background have needs and wants, as do their parents. Problems arise when the needs and wants of parents and children don't fit together like pieces of a puzzle.

The occasionally overwhelming problems of parenting can often be minimized when parents learn how to adjust their responses according to their preschoolers' needs. This book offers practical remedies for the common behavioral problems of preschoolers—remedies that parents and caregivers can apply in the heat of conflicts that arise during the course of normal family life.

Our intent is to show parents how to react to discipline problems in calm, consistent, and effective ways—without shouting or spanking. We want to help parents become "disciplined parents" who can control themselves when their children are losing control. By maintaining self-control, parents can avoid the dangers of using violence in any form, either inflicted or threatened. Shouting and spanking are forms of violence that teach children that inflicting fear and pain on others is a way to control their behavior.

The approach we take in this book—discipline as *teaching* rather than punishing—mirrors that of our original edition and combines the best of our forty collective years of professional and parental experience. We have studied and taught developmental and child psychology at the university level; served on the psychology staff of a state hospital for children; worked as a psychologist in a major suburban school district; founded five national parenting publications; conducted numerous parent groups, national seminars, and workshops; consulted with school districts and mental health centers; written extensively about parenting for radio, magazines, and newspapers, as well as the internet and other media; and raised a total of four children.

Our problem-solving principles and discipline strategies are based on behavioral psychology, which studies the behavior of children in "real" settings—homes, schools, and playgrounds. Since the publication of the first edition of *Discipline without Shouting or Spanking* in 1984, new behavioral issues have emerged. We have addressed these issues in this new edition.

- The relationship between violence in the home and violence at school.
- The link between playing with imaginary or toy guns as a preschooler and using guns in school and elsewhere.
- The spanking debate: Is moderate spanking harmful?
- The influence of electronic media (computers, internet, TV, electronic games) on behavior.
- The concern about the diagnosis of hyperactivity or Attention Deficit Hyperactivity Disorder (ADHD).
- The long-term causes and consequences of childhood obesity.
- The challenge of discipline for single parents.
- The crucial role parents play in building and maintaining empathy in children.

We have designed this book, like the original edition, to be a handy reference guide for parents and other caregivers—a first-aid handbook for managing misbehavior. We recognize parents' need for brevity, immediacy, and practicality. We offer advice on how to prevent misbehavior problems from occurring and how to solve them when they happen. We also include "case histories" that illustrate how a number of fictionalized families have used the strategies to handle real problems.

Who Is a Preschooler?

We use the term *preschool years* to describe the awesome, metamorphic days and nights during which a one-year-old child seems to suddenly become a five-year-old miniature adult. Generally speaking, *preschooler* refers to a child who hasn't reached school age (kindergarten or first grade) and includes toddlers but not infants. Newborn babies and children under one year old are unique creatures primarily governed by needs (food, sleep, and human contact) that are generally met through physical and emotional nurturing. Preschoolers' needs, on the other hand, often require psychological strategies. For this reason, this book focuses on post-infancy children whose normal development creates behavioral problems that force parents and other caregivers to adopt civilizing strategies in order to give children the tools they need to become happy, healthy human beings. The central work that is done during the pre-school years is the teaching and civilizing that prepares children for formal schooling. (See "The Transition to Elementary School for You and Your Child" on page 9.)

Note: Please read "Milestones of Development" (pages 10–11) and "The Differences between Boys and Girls" (pages 8–9) before applying the do's and don'ts in each chapter. Doing so will help you understand the general behavioral characteristics of one- to five-year-olds as well as the influence of brain structure, body chemistry, and hormones on boy-girl behavioral dissimilarities. Understanding preschooler development will help prevent you from mistaking certain behaviors as abnormal or from erroneously blaming yourself for causing your child's misbehavior. For example, in order to understand the motivations behind your two-year-old's prolific use of *no,* it helps to know that negativism is a normal part of a two-year-old's behavior. To understand why boys are generally more aggressive during their tantrums than girls, it helps to know something about biological differences between the sexes.

Introduction

The preschool years are the prime physical, emotional, and intellectual learning years of life. At their best, preschoolers are curious, inventive, eager, and independent. At their worst, they are obstinate, inhibited, and clinging. Both their chameleonlike personalities and their inability to use adult logic make them tough customers for those selling life's behavior lessons. Preschoolers live in a world that is challenging to them as well as to their parents, and teaching preschoolers—which is what disciplining really is—is sometimes like working with fertile ground and sometimes like hitting your head against a brick wall.

This should not be especially surprising. Parents and their preschoolers are usually at least twenty years apart in age and light-years apart in experience, reasoning ability, and the capacity for self-control. They also have different ideas, feelings, expectations, rules, beliefs, and values about themselves, each other, and the world. For example, children are born not knowing that it isn't acceptable to write on walls. They will only learn the desirable ways of expressing their artistic talents if their parents consistently teach them where they can write, praise them when they follow directions, and outline the consequences of breaking the rule.

At the same time, children have their own needs, desires, and feelings, most of which they cannot articulate very well. Throughout their first five years, they struggle to become independent human beings and rebel against being "raised" by older people.

The ultimate goals that parents have for their preschoolers are the immediate goals they have for themselves: self-control and self-sufficiency. It's important for parents to understand that they operate on a timetable that's different from their children's and that each child's ability to learn is unique. This understanding helps parents use empathy, trust, and respect as the foundation for healthy family communication.

The number one task facing parents of preschoolers is teaching them appropriate behavior *on a level they can understand.* When dealing with their children's temper tantrums, for example, parents are not only attempting to restore calm and order to their household, they're also trying to teach their children how to handle frustration and anger in a more appropriate way. Parents must model the kind of behavior they want to teach. They must also communicate their values in ways that make the values as important for their children as they are for themselves.

Building Emotionally Strong Children

Children who believe they are the masters of their fate, who feel they belong, and who feel competent are more likely to become strong, resilient children and adults. This fact of life is as true today as it was in 1984 when the first edition of *Discipline without Shouting or Spanking* was published. In this book and also in *How to Discipline Your Six to Twelve Year Old...Without Losing Your Mind* (Doubleday, 1991), we help you understand that children thrive in a climate in which parents:

- accept children's inborn personality and temperament;
- help them develop a sense of responsibility for their actions;
- create a loving and safe environment built on mutual trust;
- teach them decision-making and problem-solving skills;
- show them how to handle mistakes as challenges rather than as disasters.

Parenthood Is Naturally Problematic

Because childhood is naturally full of problems and conflicts, parents need to ask themselves a number of questions before labeling any of their children's behaviors a "problem."

How often does a certain kind of misbehavior occur?

And how intense is it? For example, if your child becomes angry easily, anger may be his natural reaction to disappointment. However, if he becomes so angry that he risks injuring himself or others, you need to find a way to at least reduce the intensity of his anger.

Do I tolerate my child's misbehavior?

Your biases, needs, or rules may allow you to tolerate or even find amusing some behaviors other parents find intolerable. Asking yourself "What will the neighbors think?" moves the problem outside the family. A parent who accepts what a child does at home may realize that other parents will not approve of it. The parent may then decide to do something about the misbehavior.

A child's behavior becomes an issue or a problem from the parents' point of view or from the point of view of other parents. Children, on the other hand, do not see their behavior as a problem; they simply have not yet learned more appropriate or self-controlled ways of seeking satisfaction.

In order to adequately manage the problems of their children's behavior, parents *themselves* need to become more disciplined (where *discipline* is defined as a teaching-learning process that leads to orderliness and self-control). Parental behavior must change before their children's behavior is most likely to change, and parents must become disciplined parents before their children will most likely become self-disciplined.

Discipline Issues for Single Parents

Parenting a young child alone is a very difficult job for even the most skilled parent. Not only is parenting a twenty-four-hour, seven-days-a-week job that requires infinite patience, it's also designed to be a team effort. In order to build independent, self-sufficient, loving, empathetic children, it's best for parents to work together to plan strategies, share duties, and decide on rules. But that's not always possible.

Instead of focusing on trying to control what the parent who lives in another house or even in another state does or doesn't do, each parent is best advised to develop the most efficient discipline plan that teaches responsible behaviors, encourages positive attitudes, and provides emotional strength. As with all parents, a single parent also needs to develop a support system with preschool, daycare, babysitters, and extended family at its core.

The ABCs of Disciplined Parenting

Over forty years of behavioral research and experience, drawn from theory and based on working with thousands of families, have taught us that it's important for practical as well as philosophical reasons to separate a child from her behavior when dealing with behavior problems. Calling a child who leaves her toys out a "slob" won't get the toys picked up or teach neat behavior. It may only affect the child by contributing to an unhealthy self-image and possibly becoming a self-fulfilling prophecy. It's best for the child's self-esteem to concentrate on specific, constructive ways of changing the behavior. Based on this principle, here are our ABCs:

Decide on the specific behavior you would like to change.

If you focus on specifics rather than abstracts, you'll manage better. For example, don't tell your child to be neat; explain that you want her to pick up her blocks before she goes out to play.

Praise your child's behavior.

Don't praise your child, but rather praise what she is *doing*. For example, instead of saying, "You're a good girl for sitting quietly," say, "It's good you're sitting quietly." Focus your praise or disapproval on your child's behavior, because that is what you're interested in managing.

Continue the praise as long as the new behavior needs that support.

Praising the appropriate things your child does reminds her of your expectations and reinforces your model of good behavior. Praise motivates your child to continue behaving appropriately.

Try to avoid power struggles with your children.

Using a technique like Beat-the-Clock (page 12) when you want your children to get ready for bed faster, for example, will help you reduce parent-child conflict because you're transferring authority to a neutral figure: a timer.

Be there.

This does not mean that parents must be with their children every minute of every day, but it does mean that children need fairly constant supervision. If parents do not pay close attention to their children, many behavior problems will go unnoticed and uncorrected.

Avoid being a historian.

Leave bad behavior to history and don't keep bringing it up. If your child makes an error, constantly reminding her of it will only lead to resentment and increase the likelihood of bad behavior. What's done is done. Working toward a better future makes more sense than dwelling on the past. Reminding your children of their errors only reminds them of what *not* to do; it doesn't show them what to do.

Spanking and Shouting Are Counterproductive

The principles outlined in this book represent what we as parents *should* do when we're confronted with our children's misbehavior. What we *often* do, however, is shout at or spank our children, especially if we're tired or distracted or frustrated by their failure to obey us. Shouting and spanking are quite natural responses to misbehavior—especially continued misbehavior—but they're also quite counterproductive. They *never* teach appropriate behavior, which is the number one task of parenting. In fact, they teach just the opposite:

- How to shout
- How to hit
- How to be sneaky
- How to fear
- How to be ashamed
- How to take anger out on others

All degrees of shouting and spanking—light, moderate, occasional, rarely, always—give children the wrong kind of attention. If it's the only kind they're given, they may misbehave just to get noticed. Also, parents don't always know if spanking works because they don't actually observe its effect on a child's behavior over time. Spanking as punishment simply drives bad behavior underground: It stops the behavior from happening in front of parents, but it doesn't stop it altogether. In fact, children become experts at not getting caught. Parents may even say, "Don't let me catch you doing that again!"

In the hierarchy of moral development, as defined by Lawrence Kohlberg, the lowest level is "following rules only to avoid punishment." The highest level is "following rules because they are right and good."[1] When parents spank their children for misbehavior, they stop their children at the lowest level of moral development. The children are interested in avoiding the punishment, not in doing what is good or right.

Spanking is also often the earliest experience a child has with violence. Children learn to behave in violent ways through adult example— a compelling reason to avoid spanking, particularly with the increased exposure children have to violence in the media. (See pages 101–105.) It's difficult to justify the admonition "Don't hit!" while you're hitting your child for hitting.

Children see the world in concrete terms. When they see that it's permissible for adults to hit children, they assume it must be permissible for children to hit adults or other children. Hitting begets hitting—as well as anger, revenge, and the breakdown of communication between parents and their children.

The *primary* message given when parents shout or spank is that adults are bigger, stronger, and more powerful than children and can inflict fear and pain if displeased. The resulting sense of being a victim and being powerless in the face of greater size and strength creates fear and anxiety in children, and ultimately the desire to use violence themselves when upset.

No positive consequences result from spanking. In fact, the link between the victimization of children and their subsequent anger-management problems, as discussed in the work of Jay Barrish and others,[2] further underscores the argument for creating a zero-tolerance policy regarding spanking in your home, at daycare, in preschool, and in other settings. However, creating a zero-tolerance policy should not result in criminal penalties for spanking. Instead, this policy should be a statement of your own beliefs that discipline should be a teaching system that builds appropriate behavior.

The Learned Nature of Violence

Much research has been done to identify the causes of violent behavior in children and adults. Although the results are still somewhat controversial, Dr. Lonnie Athens' work, as cited in Richard Rhodes' book *Why They Kill*,[3] presents strong evidence regarding the development of violent adults.

Dr. Athens conducted in-depth interviews with people who were imprisoned for violent behavior. The interviews revealed that children who are frequently abused, threatened with abuse, or who witness others being abused are at very high risk for learning that violence is a way to solve problems, get what they want, or protect themselves from a perceived threat. When violence accomplishes these goals, children gain reputations as "nobody messes with me" kind of people. They get glory from infamy, and violence becomes a way of life. We believe that it's vitally important for every caregiver of every child to be aware of these dangerous consequences of the use of violence in any form, either threatened or actually inflicted on a child or other person. When caregivers understand this risk, we believe they will refuse to support spanking as a discipline option.

The Importance of Empathy in Discipline

Empathy is the ability to identify with and understand another's situation, feelings, and motives. All children are born with the capacity to be empathetic. Research indicates that this ability varies from child to child as they grow, and that girls have a greater capacity than boys to read emotions. Nevertheless, by two years of age, both boys and girls are able to understand others' feelings. By four years of age, children have the ability to comprehend the reasons for others' feelings. However, if empathy is to grow and flourish, parents must nurture its development.

The most important factor in building and maintaining empathy in children is respecting their individuality by modeling empathy, understanding, and caring—regardless of how difficult a child's behavior may be to manage. For example, by beginning your response to inappropriate behavior with the statement "I'm sorry you chose to do that...," you're showing your child that you care about his feelings and have empathy for his being in the "hot seat." In addition, parents can develop their children's potential to be empathetic by pointing out the impact of their behavior on others.

Conversely, the use of shouting or spanking to manage children's behavior erodes their ability to be empathetic. When we react with anger to children's behavior, we teach them to act without considering another person's feelings—a consequence we need to avoid. Studies by JoAnn Robinson, Ph.D., of the University of Colorado,[4] support this truth. She reported that greater maternal warmth is associated with increases in children's empathy during the second year of life, but children whose mothers control them with anger show decreases in empathy. Without empathy, it's nearly impossible for children to learn to share toys, play well with others, avoid angry and violent reactions to adversity, and take personal responsibility for their actions.

Using the positive teaching strategies outlined in this book will not only help keep *your* empathy quotient high, it will also help develop your children's potential to become empathetic, loving, caring adults.

The Role of Self-Talk

We encourage parents to use what we call *self-talk* to help them avoid falling into the habit of saying irrational things to themselves. *Self-talk* is best defined as what people say to themselves that governs their behavior. For example, if a parent says, "I can't stand it when my child whines!" then that parent's level of tolerance for the whining will be greatly diminished. However, if that parent says, "I don't like it when my child whines, but I can survive it," then not only will that parent be able to tolerate the whining longer, he or she will also be more likely to plan effective ways of changing the behavior.

Self-talk should be used to set ourselves up for success rather than failure. What we say to ourselves constitutes the most important messages we receive, so self-talk is a great tool for parents of preschoolers. If parents can calm themselves in times of stress by using helpful self-talk, then they will be more likely to follow through with reasonable and responsible actions.

Sometimes parents sabotage themselves with self-talk that encourages them to "follow the crowd." For example, if your child's friend's parents let your child use a bed as a trampoline, you may feel pressured to do the same by telling yourself you won't fit into the "good-parent club" if you don't. This peer-pressure self-talk can be harmless: You buy a certain kind of peanut butter because other parents buy it. However, it can also be dangerous if it leads you to shout at or spank your child because other moms and dads do. Instead of following the crowd, we encourage you to follow your heart, your common sense, and your knowledge of the most effective and caring ways of raising responsible, self-sufficient, and empathetic children.

The Differences between Boys and Girls

To better understand your preschooler's behavior, it's helpful to understand the differences between boys and girls. This information can help you distinguish between normal behaviors and those that need to be addressed as discipline issues. Knowing the natural differences between boys and girls can also help you avoid comparing your different-sex children. (See also "Milestones of Development" on pages 10–11 for more information on preschooler development.)

Research has shown that boys and girls differ in brain structure, body chemistry, and hormones, and that these differences strongly influence boy-girl behavioral dissimilarities. For example, boys' brains develop more slowly than girls'. In boys, the left half of the brain, which controls thinking, develops more slowly than the right half, which controls spatial relationships. As a result, the connection between the two hemispheres is not as fully formed in boys, who generally enjoy greater ability in math and reasoning, but lesser ability in language and reading.

Girls' brains develop more evenly, giving them the ability to use both hemispheres for such activities as reading and emotional awareness. The female brain is at work most of the time, allowing girls to be more skilled at multi-tasking. Girls' brains also secrete more serotonin, a neurotransmitter that inhibits aggression.

On the other hand, boys' brains secrete more testosterone, a hormone that drives aggression. As a result, boys tend to seek instant gratification (eating quickly, jumping from activity to activity), to move quickly to problem-solving (even in highly emotional situations), and to engage in activities that create tension (sports, contests, and games). These tendencies allow boys to release pent-up energy.

Other common differences* between boys and girls include the following:

- Boys prefer to focus on a single task, and they react more aggressively to interruptions.
- Girls' motor activities peak less quickly, are less vigorous, and last longer.
- Boys create and play games that fill larger spaces, and they need to be outside more.
- Girls' attention to objects is less fleeting and less active.
- Girls rely more on their five senses.

- Boys do better with visual information presented to the left eye, which feeds the right hemisphere.
- By age five, girls are six months ahead of boys in general development.
- Boys who see themselves as physically strong will seek rough and tumble play.
- Boys who feel safe and competent will seek independence earlier than girls.

*These differences are broad generalizations based on the vast amount of research on the development of boys and girls. Individual children may vary from these tendencies.

The Transition to Elementary School for You and Your Child

One- to five-year-olds are referred to as *preschoolers* because this is the stage in which they become self-disciplined or "civilized" by the pre-educational process that prepares them to function in the organized and regimented world of elementary school. So who does this civilizing? Parents, childcare providers, preschool teachers, coaches, friends, extended family members, neighbors, and other adults play important roles in teaching preschoolers such virtues as empathy, patience, self-control, responsibility, respect, cooperation, courage, courtesy, perseverance, and honesty.[5]

A steady moral compass of virtues will guide children on their journey from being "little" preschoolers to "big" elementary schoolers. It's crucial for parents to carefully select their preschoolers' first teachers based on their ability to teach these virtues. Children must learn to play cooperatively and to become increasingly self-sufficient when they are separated from their moms and dads for greater amounts of time. The preschool years are the foundation for children's learning readiness.

In our book *The Eight Seasons of Parenthood* (Times Books, 2000), we describe how preschoolers' behaviors force parents to assume the identity of "Family Managers" when teaching their children appropriate behaviors. As children change from being helpless, horizontal human beings to upright, mobile, do-it-myselfers, parents move from managing their children's lives to becoming organizational wizards who juggle working, cooking, cleaning, driving, and playing—all while being their children's first and most important teachers. Becoming a mother or father is so much more than giving birth to a child. It's a developmental process that continues for the rest of a parent's life.

Milestones of Development

The following chart describes some of the milestones parents can expect their one- to five-year-olds to reach during their preschool years. These milestones are presented according to the age at which they usually occur. Since each child develops on an individual timetable, a particular child may be ahead of, on, or behind the statistical average. Consult your child's health-care professional if your child is consistently delayed in reaching milestones or if you're concerned about other aspects of your child's development.

Age	Milestones
1–2 Years	• Explores his environment; gets into things • Takes one long nap a day • Plays alone for short periods of time • Explores his body
2–3 Years	• Runs, climbs, pushes, pulls; is very active • Legs appear knock-kneed • Feeds himself with fingers, spoon, and cup • Can remove some of his clothing • Explores his genitalia • Sleeps less, wakes easily • Likes routines • Becomes upset if his mother is away overnight • Wants to do things himself • Is balky and indecisive; changes his mind • Has flashes of temper; changes his moods often • Imitates adults • Plays beside but not with children his own age • Is not yet able to share, wait, take turns, give in • Likes water play • Prolongs the good-night ritual • Uses single words, short sentences • Is often negative; says "No" • Understands more than he can say
3–4 Years	• Runs, jumps, and climbs • Feeds himself; drinks neatly from a cup • Carries things without spilling • Can help dress and undress himself • May not sleep at naptime, but plays quietly

- Is responsive to adults; wants approval
- Is sensitive to expressions of disapproval
- Cooperates; likes to run simple errands
- Is at a "Me, too!" stage; wants to be included
- Is curious about things and people
- Is imaginative; may fear the dark, animals
- May have an imaginary companion
- May get out of bed at night
- Is talkative; uses short sentences
- Can wait his turn; has a little patience
- Can take some responsibility, such as putting away toys
- Plays well alone, but group play can be stormy
- Is attached to parent of opposite sex
- Is jealous, especially of a new baby
- Demonstrates guilt feelings
- Releases emotional insecurity by whining, crying, requesting reassurance of love
- Releases tension by thumbsucking, nail biting

4–5 Years
- Continues to gain weight and height
- Continues to gain coordination
- Has good eating, sleeping, and elimination habits
- Is very active
- Starts things, but doesn't necessarily finish them
- Is bossy, boastful
- Plays with others, but is self-assertive
- Has short-lived quarrels
- Speaks clearly; is a great talker
- Tells stories; exaggerates
- Uses toilet words in a silly way
- Makes up meaningless words with lots of syllables
- Laughs, giggles
- Dawdles
- Washes when told
- Is at the "How?" and "Why?" stage
- Demonstrates dependence on peers

Discipline Dictionary

The following terms are defined according to how they are used in this book:

Beat-the-Clock

A motivational technique that uses your child's competitive nature to encourage her to complete tasks on your timetable. Here's how it works: Set a timer for the amount of time you want to allow your child to complete a task. Ask, "Can you finish before the timer rings?" Since children love to win, this allows them to win a race against time. More importantly, your child completes the task in a timely fashion without a power struggle. Our forty years of working with thousands of children and families have shown that Beat-the-Clock reduces parent-child conflicts because it transfers authority to a neutral figure: a timer.

Grandma's Rule

A contractual arrangement that follows the pattern "When you have done X (what the parent wants the child to do), then you may do Y (what the child wants to do)." Grandma's Rule is best stated in the positive rather than the negative. Never substitute "if" for "when." This encourages a child to ask, "What if I don't do X?" Grandma's Rule, which is derived from the axiom "When you work, you eat," has a powerful effect on behavior because it sets up established reinforcers (rewards, positive consequences) for appropriate behavior.

Neutral Time

Time that's free from conflict, such as the time after a tantrum is finished and your child is playing calmly. Neutral time is the best time for teaching new behavior because your child is calm and receptive to learning.

Praise

To verbally recognize a behavior you want to reinforce. Praise should always describe the behavior and not the child. For example, say, "Good eating," not "Good girl for eating." When you say, "Good girl for eating," you're doing something you don't want to do: connecting a child's worth to her behavior. You don't want to teach a child that as long as she's behaving appropriately, she's a good person—but should she make a mistake, she becomes a bad girl. We believe that children are inherently good. Their behavior is what parents are judging and striving to change for the better.

Reprimand

A short statement that includes the following: (1) a command to stop the behavior, (2) a reason why the behavior should stop, and (3) an alternative to the behavior. For example, you might say to your child, "Stop hitting. Hitting hurts people. Ask your friend nicely to give you the toy."

Rule

A predetermined behavioral expectation that includes a stated outcome and consequences. For example, one of your rules might be "We put our dirty clothes in the hamper when we take them off so we can keep our house neat and so we won't have to pick up stuff all the time. And for remembering the rule, you won't have to practice putting your dirty clothes in the hamper." Establishing and enforcing rules is an effective problem-solving technique. Our years of working with children and families have shown that children will behave more appropriately when their world has clear boundaries and when they can anticipate the consequences of their behavior.

Time Out

To take a child out of a situation for a set period of time, usually because of inappropriate behavior. A typical Time Out involves taking your child to a chair or room, setting a timer for a certain length of time (approximately one minute for each year of age, up to five minutes), and telling her she must stay there until the timer rings. If she leaves Time Out before the timer rings, reset the timer and tell her she has to stay there until the timer rings. Repeat the process until she stays in Time Out for the designated time. One of the benefits of Time Out is that it separates you from your child when tempers are flaring, giving you and your child the opportunity to regain self-control.

Using This Book

To use this book most effectively, think of each "What to Do" suggestion as a remedy for a certain behavior problem. Judge for yourself the seriousness of the problem, then begin with the least severe first-aid measure. The guiding principle for changing children's behavior is "Try the mildest strategy first." This usually means showing your child what to do and encouraging him to do it. If that doesn't work, try the next mildest strategy and proceed from there until you find something that works. It's equally important to know what *not* to do in a behavioral crisis, so pay special attention to the "What Not to Do" suggestions listed in each section. These will help you prevent certain behavior problems from recurring or becoming more severe.

Because parents and children are individuals, certain words and actions as applied in specific situations in this book will feel more natural to some than to others. Change a word or two if the exact language doesn't flow comfortably from your mouth. One- to five-year-olds are acutely aware of and sensitive to the feelings and subtle reactions of their parents. Make what you say and do believable to your children, and they will more readily accept your discipline.

The remedies in this book are designed to show your child the kind of respect you would give others in your home. Your children learn to be respectful by being treated respectfully. Treat your child as if he were a guest in your house. This does not mean your child shouldn't follow the rules; it means he should be taught in a kind and respectful way how to follow the rules.

Since 1984, this book has been the discipline framework for hundreds of thousands of parents and childcare providers. We are honored to be such an important part of the beginning chapter in families' lives. Their journey is your journey, our journey, as we nurture preschool-aged children.

Aggressive Behavior

Like bulls in china shops, many energetic preschoolers hurl toys or their bodies at the nearest targets when frustrated, angry, or rambunctious. Why? Because the little dynamos are not able to reason or compromise, and throwing books or toys doesn't seem any different from tossing balls. Tame your child's aggressive behavior by first explaining that hitting, biting, throwing, and teasing are unacceptable. Then show and tell (even your one-year-old) the kind of behavior you want your child to exhibit: kissing, hugging, talking, and so on. Also, explain why these actions are acceptable. Make sure to strictly and consistently enforce the rules in order to guide your child on the path toward appropriate behavior.

Note: If your child's aggressive behavior is a regular feature of her daily play and is disruptive to friends, family, and yourself, seek professional help to find out what may be causing this behavior.

Preventing the Problem

Closely supervise your child's play.

To prevent your child from learning aggressive behavior from her peers, monitor how she and her friends interact with each other and how they care for their toys. Don't let aggressive behavior cause injury or damage. Also, treat your child's friends' misbehavior as you would your child's.

Don't model aggressive behavior.

Treat your things they way you'd like your children to treat theirs. For example, hitting or throwing things when you're angry shows your child how to be aggressive when she's mad.

Explain why biting and hitting are unacceptable.

To help your child understand just how unpleasant aggressive behavior is for both sides, explain how biting and hitting make the victim feel.

Solving the Problem

What to Do

Tell your child what to do besides hit.

When aggressive behavior starts, tell your child things to do besides hit when she's feeling upset. For example, tell her she may ask for help or say, "I'm not playing anymore," or she may simply leave the playgroup. Ask her to practice these lines five times until she's familiar with the words and how to use them.

Compliment getting along.

Explain what you mean by *getting along* by telling your child you appreciate her behavior when she shares, takes turns, asks for help, and so on. For example, say, "Good sharing with your friends, honey." Always be specific about what you're praising. The more you praise your child's behavior, the more it will be repeated.

Use reprimands.

Reprimanding your child helps her understand why you disapprove of her behavior. It also shows that you respect your child's ability to understand your reasons. The three parts of an effective reprimand for hitting, for example, include telling your child to stop ("Stop hitting!"), explaining why you disapprove ("Hitting hurts people!"), and suggesting an acceptable alternative to hitting ("When you're angry, just leave the group."). If your child continues to be aggressive, repeat the reprimand and include a Time Out to reinforce your message.

Forget the incident when it's over.

Reminding your child of her previous aggressions doesn't teach her acceptable behavior. On the contrary, it reminds her of how she could be aggressive again.

What Not to Do

Don't use aggression to stop aggression.

Hitting your child only gives her permission to hit others in similar circumstances.

Don't let off steam when your child does.

Getting angry when your child hits, for example, only proves to your child that she can use aggression to get power over you.

Mike the Biter

At twenty-two months of age, Mike Morgan became known as the neighborhood biter, having had lots of practice on his two older brothers, who teased him mercilessly. Mrs. Morgan threatened her youngest child in order to stop his aggressiveness. "If you don't stop biting people, Mikey, I'm going to spank you." But she knew she never intended to back up her threat.

Mike's three- and five-year-old brothers' teasing didn't seem to bother their mother. In fact, her family joked frequently about lots of things, and she considered the older boys' making fun of Mikey all in the spirit of not taking yourself too seriously. Her husband didn't agree. "Think how all that teasing must make Mike feel," he said one day.

Though she didn't want to admit it, Mrs. Morgan had never thought about this problem from Mike's point of view—that he got back at his brothers by biting because he couldn't match their verbal attacks. She decided to teach all three boys that biting, hitting, teasing, and throwing things would not be tolerated. She believed that this was the only way to teach the older boys to model good behavior and to teach Mike to make better choices about how to get attention.

The next day, Mike began to bite his brothers after they called him "little Oscar the Grouch." Mrs. Morgan reprimanded Mike first. "Stop biting, Mikey. Biting hurts people. We bite apples, not people." She also reprimanded Mike's brothers. "Stop teasing. We do not tease people. It hurts their feelings."

But the reprimands didn't stop the boys' verbal and physical attacks. So Mrs. Morgan said, "I'm sorry you're still biting and teasing each other. Time Out!" The three boys were then directed to separate chairs and told to think about what happened and to think about ways in which they could avoid having it happen again.

As Mrs. Morgan became consistent in her discipline, and as she praised any getting along the boys did within the home, the Morgan boys learned what to expect from fighting and from being friendly. Mike began to bite less, since he didn't have to tolerate his brothers' teasing, and the older boys learned that teasing was hurtful.

Behaving Shyly

Imagine seeing your neighbor at the supermarket as you're happily shopping with your three-year-old son. Suddenly, he clutches your leg and won't answer your neighbor's simple greeting, "How are you, Sam?" You're surprised at this odd behavior and ask your son, "What's the problem? You love Kathy!"

You're not alone. Millions of parents are confused by their children's "freezing up" when confronted with questions. While some children approach the world with unbridled curiosity, others keep tight rein on their inquisitiveness, choosing to "look before they leap." Both tendencies are considered normal, each reflecting an innate style.

In other words, shyness is not a problem in and of itself. However, it becomes a problem when a child's shyness becomes so powerful that it prevents him from making friends or participating in social activities away from home, such as going to a birthday party or the library. Teaching social skills and role-playing various social situations will help preschoolers reduce their shyness and increase their self-confidence.

Preventing the Problem

Develop realistic expectations and goals.

How you expect your child to act around other people may not be realistic given his developmental stage. For example, if your two-year-old isn't ready to go to a birthday party, forcing him to go will only create more fear about future social events. Preschoolers overcome their shyness as they gain experience interacting with others. However, don't expect changes overnight.

Accept your child's shyness.

Children are born with different temperaments: Some are friendly and outgoing, some are cautious and shy, and some bounce back and forth between the two. Instead of sending your shy child the message that something's wrong with him because he doesn't act according to your expectations, accept his shyness as part of his unique temperament.

Compliment your child.

When your child makes a comment during a conversation, pay him a compliment. For example, say, "I like what you said about the puppy, Stevie. He does have an unusual white paw."

Be a good role model.

Give your child plenty of opportunities to watch you interact with people in social situations. Also, role-play different scenarios with your child, teaching him what to say in certain situations. For example, say, "When people ask me how I feel, I usually say, 'Fine. How are you?'"

Solving the Problem

What to Do

Provide an environment that's free from blame and shame.

When your child feels he can make mistakes without being blamed or shamed, he can more easily give up his shy ways. If your child spills his milk, say, "That's no big deal. Here, we can clean it up together."

Practice responding to questions.

If your child shifts into shy mode, he's probably telling you he needs to be taught how to answer questions. Practice with him while you're riding in the car or playing in the bathtub. For example, say, "When somebody says, 'What's your name?' say, 'Stevie.' That way they'll know who you are. Now, let's practice. When I say, 'What's your name?' what do you say?" Practice with your child several times each day until "Stevie" is the automatic response.

Practice with family and friends.

Provide your child opportunities to participate in conversations. For example, say, "What do you think about having pizza for dinner tonight?" or, "Tell Johnny about your trip to the zoo today."

Seek professional help if necessary.

If shyness is interfering with your child's happiness, if it keeps him from participating in appropriate activities, and if it seems to be making him miserable, you should seek help from a qualified professional.

What Not to Do

Don't humiliate or punish.

Even though you may feel embarrassed by your child's shyness, punishing or humiliating him will further discourage him from becoming socially confident. Apologizing for his behavior by telling others he's "your shy child" or he "doesn't speak" will only deepen his fear of others.

Don't beg.

Although you may be sorely tempted to beg your child to "answer the nice lady," doing so will give your child's reticence considerable power and will encourage more refusals in the future.

Don't label.

Making excuses to family and friends by saying your child is "shy" creates a self-fulfilling prophecy he has to live up to. It also discourages him from trying to behave differently in the future.

Getting to Know Eduardo

Eduardo Bartone had been a shy baby who would turn his face away from strangers or bury his head in his mother's shoulder when strangers were around. His dad, Miguel, had also been shy as a child. Eduardo's Grandma Leona said that no one outside the family heard Miguel talk until he was almost a teenager.

Eduardo's mother, Maria, had hoped that Eduardo would outgrow his shyness. But at five years old, "Timido" Eduardo, as she called him, showed no signs of becoming more outgoing. Miguel understood his son and the pain he felt when he was confronted with talking to strangers.

So Miguel worked out a plan to help his son. First he engaged him in conversation by asking lots of questions that Eduardo had to answer with more than a yes or no. Miguel asked his son, "What did you have for lunch today?" or, "What games did you play at preschool today?" When Eduardo answered with more than one or two words, Miguel would say, "Eduardo, I'm glad you told me about that," or, "That was a really interesting story about playing airplane on the playground."

Miguel also had Eduardo practice greeting people. The two would pretend they were meeting on the street, and Eduardo would say, "Hello, how are you?" Miguel would answer, "Fine, thank you. And you?" Then they would both laugh. Eventually, Eduardo began to relax more around people he didn't know well, and family and friends started to comment on how polite he was becoming.

Eduardo's mom and dad were happy for him. They had expected him to follow Miguel's timid path, and they were thrilled to see him coming out of his shell. They pledged to each other that they would never again put a label on their son.

Being a Couch Potato

In today's world of high-tech, low-energy toys and games, your child can easily let her fingers—not her legs—do the walking. However, young children need physical activity to develop their muscles and minds. Resist the urge to buy yourself some free time by constantly plunking your preschooler in front of an electronic babysitter. Parent-approved computer and video games and educational television programs can be constructive teaching tools. However, if used excessively, they can lay the foundation for an unhealthy, sedentary lifestyle.

Preventing the Problem

Turn off the TV.

The American Academy of Pediatrics recommends that parents restrict the amount of children's television viewing to less than two hours per day. Limiting television viewing and other "couch" activities encourages children's creativity and reduces aggressiveness.

Get moving!

Physical activities stimulate the heads and hearts of both children and parents. Playing jumping jacks, galloping horses, and other fun physical games tones your toddlers' muscles and also tires the little ones out so they sleep more soundly.

Cultivate creativity.

Instead of letting your preschoolers become passive media sponges, focus their attention on building forts, inventing games, drawing pictures, creating collages, and doing other creative activities to keep their growing minds and bodies active.

Solving the Problem

What to Do

Set time limits on using electronic media.

To avoid habitual media overindulgence, set a timer to tell your child when it's time to click the off button, and praise her when she turns to more physical activities. Say, "I'm glad you turned off the TV and chose to play school. What are you teaching this morning?"

Show your children how to be active.

Children are professional imitators, so showing them how to stay active means staying active yourself. If they see you cooking, cleaning, washing, writing, exercising, visiting with friends, paying bills, working outside, and playing with them, they'll be encouraged to use their time interacting with their world instead of watching TV.

Praise activity.

When your children are engaged in active play, point out their healthy behavior by saying, "Swinging is fun, and it helps your body and mind grow healthy and strong."

What Not to Do

Don't use the TV to buy child-free time.

Telling your child to "go watch TV and stay out of the kitchen while I'm fixing dinner" only encourages her to be a couch potato. Instead of banishing your child from the kitchen, introduce her to the world of broiling, baking, and boiling by asking her to do age-appropriate tasks such as washing the potatoes or tearing up the lettuce.

Don't reward with food.

Help your child learn that food is to be used for nourishment, not as a reward for good behavior or as something to soothe a broken heart. Keep your praise food-free, so that your giving food is not confused with giving approval or love.

Don't allow eating in front of the TV.

Linking watching TV with snacking can cause couch potatoes to "fluff up" in an unhealthy manner! Moreover, when your child eats while watching TV, she isn't able to focus properly on either activity, and she misses the value of each.

A Weighty Problem

Latisha Johnson's favorite pastime was watching television, but a close second was playing video games on the family computer. The fact that she was occupied for hours was both good and bad for her mother, Janelle. The good news? Janelle could make dinner after work without interruptions because Latisha would race for her beloved electronic toys as soon as she got home from daycare. The bad news? Latisha's massive doses of media were becoming hazardous to her health.

Not only did the four-year-old love watching TV, she also loved eating while watching. She begged Janelle to buy all the junk food advertised on TV, and Janelle, hating to upset her daughter, obliged. However, Janelle started to feel guilty when the pediatrician mentioned how much weight Latisha had gained since her last checkup.

Unfortunately, Latisha wasn't the only one who loved TV and junk food. Anthony, Latisha's dad, was an inveterate "couch potato." He came home from work and plunked himself on the sofa, where he watched ball game after ball game. Anthony understood the problem his daughter was developing because he knew how hard it was to get a belt buckled around his ever-growing middle.

One night at dinner, Janelle said, "Latisha, sweetheart, your dad and I think that we all watch too much TV around here, so we've made three new rules. First, we're going to allow only one hour of TV each day, and we'll decide as a family what to watch. Second, the computer will be used for only one hour each day. Third, we'll eat in the kitchen or dining room, and we won't have TV on during that time."

"But I like TV!" Latisha whined. "What can I do if I can't watch TV or play games on the computer?"

"I have an idea," Anthony said. "Let's make up our own television shows. We'll get costumes, imagine stories, and become actors."

"Oh, yes!" Latisha said excitedly. So that night they rummaged through the house gathering old clothes for costumes and designing a set in the basement. They worked so hard that Latisha was exhausted when she went to bed that night. Every week after that she invited her preschool friends over to play "TV Show" in the basement.

Janelle not only saw her plump little girl begin to slim down, she also noticed how creative Latisha was becoming in so many different ways. Latisha was also becoming more interested in being read to at bedtime, instead of insisting that they watch TV together before she went to sleep. The family's creative play was the perfect diet for Anthony, too. His middle started firming up when he started hosting an exercise class for their home "TV Show."

Although Janelle had lost her free time to family time, she realized that the change was good for everyone. She knew that the rewards of talking, laughing, loving, and growing closer far outweighed the sacrifice.

Clinging to Parents

The image of a preschooler clutching his mother's skirt, hanging on for dear life while she tries to cook or walk out the door, is not make-believe for many parents. It's a real and emotionally draining part of everyday life. Though it may be tough, resist the temptation to constantly attend to your clinging vine as you go about your day. If you want (or need) to leave your child with a babysitter, firmly and lovingly reassure him by telling him that you're proud of him for staying with the sitter and that you will return. Tell him in a sincere voice that you're happy he has the chance to play with the babysitter. Your positive attitude will be contagious (as would a negative one). You'll also be a good model for feeling okay about being separated and having a good time with other people. Provide lots of hugs and kisses during neutral times, to prevent him from feeling ignored and needing to cling to you to get attention. Clinging, unlike hugging, is an urgent demand for immediate attention.

Preventing the Problem

Practice leaving your child with a sitter.

To get your child used to the idea that you may not always be around, practice leaving him occasionally for short periods of time (a few hours) early in his life. These breaks are healthy for both parents and children.

Tell your child what you'll both be doing in your absence.

Telling your child what you'll be doing while you're gone gives him a good example to follow when you ask him to talk about his day's activities. Describe what he'll be doing and where you'll be while you're away, so he won't worry about his fate or yours. For example, say, "Laura will fix your dinner, read you a story, and tuck you into bed. Your daddy and I are going out to dinner, and we'll be back at eleven o'clock tonight." Or say, "I need to cook dinner now. When I've done that and you've played with Play-Doh, then we can read a story together."

Play Peek-a-Boo.

This simple game gets your child used to the idea that things (and you) go away and, more importantly, come back. Toddlers and preschoolers play Peek-a-Boo in a variety of ways: by hiding behind their hands or some object, by watching others hide behind their hands or some object, and (for two- to five-year-olds) by engaging in a more physically active game of Hide-and-Seek.

Reassure your child that you'll be coming back.

Don't forget to tell him that you'll be returning, and prove to him you're as good as your word by coming back when you said you would.

Create special "sitter" activities.

"Activity treats" help your child look forward to staying with a sitter instead of being upset by your absence. Set aside special videos, finger-paints, games, storybooks, and so on that only come out with a sitter.

Prepare your child for the separation.

Tell your child that you'll be leaving and plant the suggestion that he can cope while you're gone. For example, say, "You're getting to be such a big boy. I know you'll be fine while I'm gone." If you surprise him by leaving without warning, he may always wonder when you're going to disappear suddenly again.

Solving the Problem

What to Do

Prepare yourself for noise when you separate and your child doesn't like it.

Remember that the noise will eventually subside when your child learns the valuable lesson that he can survive without you for a brief time. Tell yourself, "He's crying because he loves me. But he needs to learn that although I can't always play with him and I occasionally go away, I'll always come back."

Praise your child for handling a separation well.

Make your child proud of his ability to play by himself. For example, say, "I'm so proud of you for entertaining yourself while I clean the oven." This will further reinforce his self-confidence and independence, which will benefit both of you.

Use the whining chair (pages 147–149).

Let your child know that it's okay for him not to like your being busy or leaving, even for short periods of time. However, make it clear that his whining disturbs others. For example, say, "I'm sorry you don't like my having to cook dinner now. Go to the whining chair until you can play without whining." Let a whining child whine—away from you.

Recognize that your child needs time away from you.
Breaks from constant companionship are necessary for children and parents. So keep your daily routine, even if your child protests your doing something besides playing with him or fusses when you occasionally leave him with a babysitter.

Start separations slowly.
If your child demands too much of your time from age one and up, play Beat-the-Clock. Give him five minutes of your time and five minutes to play by himself. Keep increasing the play-by-himself time for each five minutes of time spent with you, until he can play by himself for one hour.

What Not to Do

Don't get upset when your child clings.
Tell yourself your child prefers your company to anything in the whole world.

Don't punish your child for clinging.
Instead, follow the steps outlined above to teach him how to separate.

Don't give mixed messages.
Don't tell your child to go away while you're holding, patting, or stroking him. This will confuse him about whether to stay or go.

Don't make sickness a convenient way to get special attention.
Don't make being sick more fun than being well by letting your sick child do things that are normally unacceptable. Sickness should be dealt with in a matter-of-fact way with few changes in routine.

"Don't Leave Me!"

Natalie and Rick Gordon loved the party circuit so much that when their four-year-old son, Tyler, clutched both their jackets in horror when a babysitter arrived, both parents discounted his feelings. "Oh come on, Tyler, honey, don't be a baby! We love you. It's silly for you to feel bad. We go out every Saturday."

But Tyler wasn't comforted. He screamed at the top of his lungs, "Don't go! Don't leave! Take me!" His clinging persisted, and the Gordons couldn't understand what they were doing wrong to make their son "punish" them whenever they wanted to leave the house. They asked themselves, "Does he hate us that much, to embarrass us in front of the babysitter and stain our party clothes with sticky fingers?"

The Gordons eventually related their frustration to their friends, the Reillys, who tried to reassure them by explaining that Tyler clung to them because he *loved* them, not because he *hated* them. The Reillys also related how they had helped their daughter adjust to their absence.

The Gordons tried the Reillys' strategy the following Saturday night. Before leaving, they prepared Tyler for their upcoming departure by saying, "You're such a big boy, now. You'll have fun playing with Laura while we're at the movies. We'll be back after you're in bed, but we'll be here in the morning when you wake up. Laura will make you popcorn in our new popcorn maker, she'll read you a story, and then you'll go to bed. Have fun!" They didn't drag out their exit with tearful hugs, and they left Tyler while he was only whimpering.

After this apparent success, they began to praise Tyler about how quiet he was being during their explanation of where they were going, what they were planning to do, and how long they'd be gone. Whenever they got a good report from the babysitter, they'd let Tyler know how proud they were of him for playing nicely while they were gone. "Thanks for being so calm and for helping Laura make the krispy treats last night," they'd say with a hug.

The Gordons were also patient. They knew they might have to wait several weeks before being able to leave to the sounds of happy feet instead of stomping and wailing. But in the meantime, they stopped verbally attacking Tyler for any "babyish" behavior, and they reduced his crying by ignoring it.

Dawdling

Because time has no meaning to a child under six years old, hurrying has no great advantages. Disguise urging your child to "come on" or "please hurry" by running races with her or by giving her chances to run to your arms. Turn instructions into fun, not frustrating orders. Let your child feel she's in control of how slow or fast she does things, so she won't need to dawdle to exert influence over the pace of events.

Preventing the Problem

Try to be an on-time person.
Tuning in to being on time helps your child understand the importance of meeting time goals and builds empathy for others. Saying "We must hurry to get ready so we can be at preschool on time and not keep your teacher waiting" motivates your child to move more quickly and makes the connection between being on time and the impact of lateness on others.

Try to allow lead time.
If you're in a hurry, waiting for your preschool tortoise may lead you to lose your cool and be that much later. Make every effort to allow enough time to get ready for outings, understanding that dawdling is a typical response to movement by someone who doesn't understand what hurrying means and is a full-time world investigator.

Establish and maintain a schedule.
Since a child needs routine and consistency in her daily life and tends to dawdle more when her routine is broken, establish time limits and a regular pattern of eating, playing, bathing, and sleeping, to familiarize her with the time frame on which you want her to operate.

Solving the Problem

What to Do

Make it easy for your child to move at your pace.
Ask motivating questions and play simple games to disguise hurrying. For example, encourage your child to get ready by having her guess what

Grandma has at her house. Or, ask your child to run to your arms if you want her to hurry along the path to your car.

Play Beat-the-Clock.

Children always move more quickly while trying to beat a timer (a neutral authority) than while trying to do what you ask. Say, "Let's see if you can get dressed before the timer rings."

Offer incentives for speed.

For example, say, "When you beat the timer, then you may play for ten minutes before we leave for school." This lets your child see for herself that good things come to those who stay on a schedule.

Reward movement as well as results.

Motivate your child to complete a task by encouraging her along the way. For example, say, "I like the way you're getting dressed so quickly," rather than waiting until she's done and only saying, "Thank you for getting dressed."

Use manual guidance.

You may need to physically guide your child through the task at hand (getting in the car, getting dressed, and so on) to teach her that the world goes on regardless of her agenda at the moment.

Use Grandma's Rule.

If your child is dawdling because she wants to do something while you want her to do something else, use Grandma's Rule. For example, say, "When you've finished getting dressed, then you may play with your train."

What Not to Do

Don't lose control.

If you're in a hurry and your child is not, don't slow both of you down even more by giving her attention for dawdling (nagging or screaming at her to get going, for example). Getting angry will only encourage your child's easygoing pace.

Don't nag.

Nagging your child to hurry up when she's dawdling only gives her attention for *not* moving. Disguise a hurry-up technique by turning it into a game.

Don't dawdle yourself.

Getting your child ready to go somewhere only to have her wait for you tells her that you don't really mean what you say. Don't announce that you're ready to go to Grandma's house, for example, when you're not.

Dawdling Allison

Three-year-old Allison had a knack for noticing blades of grass or toying with her shoestrings instead of doing what was necessary at the moment. Grandma Harris, her daily babysitter, felt bad about having to get angry and nearly drag her granddaughter to the preschool door. "Hurry! Stop dawdling!" she would command, but Allison was oblivious to any encouragement to do things faster than she wanted.

Feeling helpless, angry, and resentful toward her favorite granddaughter, Grandma Harris finally told her daughter that she could no longer care for Allison. Mrs. Smith advised her mother to praise Allison's attempts at not dawdling and to ignore her when she dawdled. Mrs. Smith also encouraged her mother to offer Allison rewards for hurrying, something that came naturally to Grandma Harris, who enjoyed bringing her grandchildren presents.

"I'm glad you're getting to the door ahead of me today," Grandma Harris said to Allison as she walked toward preschool more quickly than usual. When Allison slowed to her normal pace as they neared the school, Grandma Harris decided to encourage her instead of complaining about her dawdling. "When you've scurried up the walkway toward the preschool before I can count to five, I'll give you that comb you saw in my purse." Allison hustled as if she'd never dawdled in her life.

Grandma Harris followed through with the comb and saw for herself the impact that rewards had on getting her granddaughter to do what she wanted her to do. Allison still had to be coaxed into dressing on her grandmother's timetable, but Grandma Harris began to enjoy her grandchild again, and she felt more in control of the time frame in which they would both operate.

Demanding Freedom

Immersed in pushing their way out into the world, preschoolers may need to be pulled back to safety because they're not as self-sufficient, self-reliant, and self-controlled as they think. As your one-year-old grows, your apron strings will gradually stretch to accommodate him. However, let him go only as far as you know is safe. Get to know your child's limits by testing his maturity and responsibility before making the mistake of allowing more freedom than he can safely handle. Allow him freedoms that are commensurate with his abilities, and give him frequent opportunities to reinforce your belief that he's mature enough to handle those freedoms.

Preventing the Problem

Establish limits and communicate them clearly.

Your child needs to know his limits before he can be expected to do what you want him to do. Even a one-year-old should be told what's "legal," to prevent as many "illegal" actions as possible.

Let your child know when he can cross the boundaries.

Reduce the attraction of certain no-no's by showing and telling your young adventurer how he can do what he wants without getting in trouble for it. For example, say, "You can cross the street, but you must hold my hand."

Allow as much freedom as your child shows he can safely handle.

If your child shows he is responsible within the limits, extend them a little. Let him know why they've changed, to help him feel good about his ability to follow directions and be responsible enough to earn freedom. Say, "Because you always tell me before you go to your friend's house next door, you can now go up the street, too. Always ask me before you go, of course."

Solving the Problem

What to Do

Offer rewards for staying within limits.

Encourage your child to stay within the limits by rewarding him for doing so. Say, "I'm happy you stayed at the swing set instead of going into the neighbor's yard. Now you may swing for three more minutes."

Establish consequences for not respecting limits.

Teach your child that not heeding your limits brings his fun to a stop. Say, "I'm sorry you left the yard. Now you must stay in the house." Or, "I'm sorry you crossed the street. Now you must stay in the backyard."

Be consistent.

Make sure you enforce the consequences every time your child breaks a rule. This teaches him you mean what you say. It also helps him feel more secure about his actions when he's away from you, because he'll clearly know what you expect him to do.

What Not to Do

Don't spank your child for going into the street.

Spanking encourages your child to hide from you while doing what you punished him for. Children who sneak into the street are in great danger, of course, so don't add to the problem by making them want to do it on the sly.

Ashley on Her Own

Five-year-old Ashley Hamilton was the most popular little girl on Twelfth Street, a situation that also caused her behavior to be the biggest problem in the Hamilton family. At breakfast one morning, Ashley told her mother, "Today, I'm going to walk to school with Susie, then I'm going to Donna's house after lunch, and then I'm going to play dolls with Maria." When her mother told Ashley she couldn't go anywhere anytime she pleased, Ashley pleaded, "Why? Why not? I'm going anyway! You can't stop me!"

These kinds of rebellious statements encouraged angry name-calling episodes between Ashley and her parents, who couldn't decide where freedom should be given and boundaries drawn to protect their "baby" from

*dangers she wasn't old enough to handle. Because Ashley was constantly get-
ting invitations, the Hamiltons couldn't ignore the problem of deciding
where and when she could go.*

*They decided to establish rules that could be changed depending on how
Ashley managed her freedom and responsibility. The Hamiltons clearly
explained these rules to Ashley, who was more than happy to learn how to
get more freedom.*

*One of the things Ashley needed to learn was how to cross the street. So
Mrs. Hamilton took her to the curb and began teaching her street-crossing
behavior: how to stop at the curb, look to the left, look to the right, and not
only look but see. Mrs. Hamilton asked Ashley to describe what she saw to
the left and right.*

*When Mrs. Hamilton was sure the street was clear, she instructed her
daughter to cross the street only when holding her hand. They crossed the
street together, looking left and right and describing what they saw. Mrs.
Hamilton praised her daughter for following directions perfectly. After ten
practices, Mrs. Hamilton said, "Ashley, let me watch you cross the street on
your own."*

*When Ashley demonstrated that she could follow directions on her own,
Mrs. Hamilton announced the new rule: "You may cross the street to go to
your friend's house, but you must come tell me first. I will come with you to
watch you."*

*Mrs. Hamilton thought this compromise was a lot of work, but she real-
ized that the only way she would feel comfortable loosening her apron
strings was if she knew her daughter could handle the responsibilities that
freedom required. Establishing and practicing the conditions of freedom
allowed everyone to feel safe, secure, and satisfied with the limits and expectations.*

Demanding to Do Things Themselves

"**M**e do it!" is one of the lines parents of preschoolers can expect to hear starting around a child's second birthday. This declaration of independence provides a golden opportunity for parents to allow their young try-it-alls to perfect their skills, as long as household rules aren't broken. Parents should remind themselves of their ultimate goal: to produce self-confident and self-sufficient children. So dig deep for extra patience as you bear with your child's mistakes, and balance the need to get chores done against the importance of teaching your preschoolers important living skills.

Preventing the Problem

Don't assume your child can't do something.
Keep track of your child's changing levels of expertise. Make sure you've given her a chance to try something before doing it for her, so you don't underestimate her current ability.

Buy clothing your child can manage.
Buy clothes that easily go up and down for your child in potty training, for example. Buy shirts that will go over her head and not get stuck on her shoulders when she puts on her clothes.

Store clothing in coordinated, accessible units.
Help your child develop an eye for coordination by sorting her clothes. Make them accessible by putting them in bins or drawers she can easily reach.

Prevent frustration.
Try to make tasks as easy for your child to accomplish as possible. Undo the snaps on her pants or start the zipper on her coat, for example, before you let her finish the job.

Solving the Problem

What to Do

Play Beat-the-Clock.

Tell your child how much time you have for a certain activity, so she won't think it's her inability to do something that makes you take over the job. Set a timer for the number of minutes you want to allow for the task, and say, "Let's see if we can get dressed before the timer rings." This helps your child learn a sense of being on time, and it reduces the power struggle between you and your child because you're not telling her to do something, the timer is. If you're in a hurry and must finish a task your child has started, explain the circumstances before taking over, to prevent your child from thinking it was her inability that made you take over.

Suggest cooperation and sharing.

Because your child doesn't understand why she can't do something, and she doesn't realize that she'll be able to do it eventually, suggest sharing a job by having her do what she can while you do the rest. For example, when tying shoes for a one-year-old, say, "Why don't you hold your sock while I'll put on your shoe." Whenever possible, let your child accomplish some portion of the task instead of merely watching you and feeling inadequate.

Make effort count.

As your child's first and most important teacher, you can encourage her to attempt various tasks. Teach her the axiom that "practice makes perfect" by saying, for example, "I like the way you tried to braid your hair. That was a great try. You can try again later, too." Or praise your child's attempt at putting on her shoes, even if she does it incorrectly.

Remain as calm and patient as you can.

If your child wants to do everything ("*I'll* put on my shorts," "*I'll* open the door," "*Me* close the drawer,"), remember that she's asserting her independence, not her obstinacy. Since you want her to learn to do things by herself, let her try. Avoid getting upset when things aren't done as quickly or precisely as you'd like. Instead, take delight in the fact that your child is taking the first step toward being self-sufficient and be proud of her for taking the initiative.

Allow as much independence as possible.

Let your child do as much by herself as she can, so frustration doesn't replace her innate curiosity. While tying her shoe, for example, don't insist on keeping her other shoe away from her fidgety fingers if she wants to hold it. She can hand it to you when you're finished with the first.

Ask your child to do things; don't demand.

To make your preschooler more likely to ask for things nicely, show her how to make requests politely. Say, "When you ask me nicely, I'll let you do X." Then explain what you mean by *nicely*. For example, tell your child to say, "Please, may I get a fork?" when she wants a fork.

What Not to Do

Don't punish your child's mistakes.

There are bound to be a few mishaps along the way, so be patient. If your child tries to pour the milk herself and accidentally spills it, help her do so more carefully the next time. Don't expect success right away.

Don't criticize your child's effort.

Avoid pointing out your child's mistakes. If she puts her sock on inside out, for example, simply say, "Let's put the smooth side of the sock inside next to your foot, okay?"

Don't feel rejected.

Don't feel hurt because your child doesn't appreciate your help. She's trying to do things on her own, and your help may be perceived as an obstacle. If she says, "Let me open the door," let her do it. She knows you can do things faster and with less effort, but she wants and needs to develop her skills. Appreciate her efforts to do things on her own.

Independent Jasmine

During the first three years of Jasmine Manning's life, her mother did everything for her. Now "Miss Independence" wanted her mother to do nothing for her, a personality change that was confusing and frustrating for Mrs. Manning. "I can't stand waiting for you, Jasmine!" Mrs. Manning would say when they were late for preschool and Jasmine would insist on putting her coat on by herself. "You're not old enough to do that by yourself."

The waves of demanding and refusing to comply began to subside when Mrs. Manning realized that the problem was causing her to dislike Jasmine and her desire to do things herself. One morning while Jasmine was dressing to go outside, Mrs. Manning noticed Jasmine putting on her coat perfectly for the first time. "That's great the way you put on your coat," Mrs. Manning said. "You're really hurrying to get ready for school! I'm so proud of you!" Jasmine let her mother finish the zipper without putting up a fight, something that hadn't happened in weeks.

As they rode to school, Mrs. Manning realized how independent her daughter was becoming. Jasmine's preschool teacher also noticed how she wanted to answer questions and be "the helper" without being told. Mrs. Manning decided she would try to adjust to Jasmine's overwhelming desire to be self-sufficient.

The next day, Jasmine wanted to set the table by herself, as usual. Instead of sending her the message that she couldn't do the job, Mrs. Manning tried to encourage Jasmine's independence while meeting her own agenda: getting the table set in short order. She announced, "Jasmine, you can set the table yourself until the timer rings. When it goes off, it's time for me to help you."

Jasmine wasn't eager for her mother's assistance, but she loved the idea of beating the timer. She was extra proud of herself for completing the job before the bell sounded. Jasmine's mother was proud, too. "That's great the way you set the table by yourself," she remarked while silently shifting the spoons to their place beside, not inside, the bowls.

Mrs. Manning continued to praise her daughter's efforts toward independence. She also made it as easy as possible for Jasmine to complete her tasks, and they began to work together to finish jobs when necessary.

Destroying Property

The line between destructive and creative play is not drawn for preschoolers until parents etch it in stone for them. So before your child reaches his first birthday, draw the line by telling (and showing) him what he can and cannot paint, tear up, or take apart. This will prevent your budding artist from doing unintentional damage to his and others' property. Consistently teach your child to be proud of and to care for his things, and let his creative juices flow in appropriate ways such as on drawing paper (not wallpaper) or with a take-apart play phone (not your real phone).

Preventing the Problem

Provide toys that are strong enough to be investigated but not destroyed.

It's natural for preschoolers to try to take apart and put together toys that lend themselves to this kind of activity (as well as ones that don't). In order to stimulate the kind of creative play you want to encourage, fill your child's play area with toys he can *do* something with (like stacking toys, push-button games, and so on) instead of ones that just sit there (like stuffed animals).

Give him plenty of things to wear and tear.

Provide lots of old clothes and materials for papier-mâché, dress-up, painting, or other activities, so your preschooler won't substitute new or valuable items for his play projects.

Communicate specific rules about caring for and playing with toys.

Young children don't innately know the value of things or how to play with everything appropriately, so teach them, for example, to use crayons on coloring books instead of newspapers and novels. Say, "Your coloring book is the only thing you can color on with crayons. Nothing else is for crayons." With regard to other destructive behavior, say, "Books are not for tearing. If you want to tear, ask me and I'll give you something." Or, "This wax apple does not come apart and cannot be eaten like a real one. If you'd like to eat an apple, please ask me and I'll give you one."

Supervise your child's play and be consistent.

Don't confuse your child and make him test the legal waters over and over by letting him destroy something he shouldn't. He won't know what to expect and won't understand when you destroy his fun by reprimanding him for a no-no that was formerly a yes-yes.

Remind him about caring.

Increase your chances of keeping destruction to a minimum by letting your child know when he's taking wonderful care of his toys. This reminds him of the rule, helps him feel good about himself, and makes him proud of his possessions.

Solving the Problem

What to Do

Overcorrect the mess.

If your child is over two years old, teach him to take care of his things by having him help clean up the messes he makes. For example, if he writes on the wall, he must clean up not only the writing but all the walls in the room. This overcorrection of the problem gives your child a sense of ownership and caring. (It also teaches him how to clean walls!)

Use reprimands.

If your child is under two years old, briefly reprimand him (tell him what he did wrong, why it was wrong, and what he should have done instead) to help him understand why he's been taken away from his fun.

Put your child in Time Out.

If you've given your child a reprimand and he destroys property again, repeat the reprimand and put him in Time Out.

What Not to Do

Don't overreact.

If your child breaks something, don't throw a tantrum yourself. Your anger communicates the idea that you care more for your things than your child. Make sure your degree of disappointment over something being destroyed isn't out of proportion to what happened.

Don't overly punish.

Just because your child damaged something valuable to you doesn't give you permission to damage your child. Rather than putting him in jail, put the valuable item away until he's old enough to understand the value.

Tim the Terror

Walt and Becky Brady knew they had a destructive three-year-old long before the preschool teacher called them in for a conference. They could have bent the teacher's ear with tales of purple crayon on the yellow dining-room wallpaper and mosaics made out of pages from hardcover books.

When the Bradys arrived home from their conference, the babysitter reported that Tim had drawn on the tile floor with his crayons. "When are you going to stop all this destruction, Tim?" Mr. Brady screamed as he spanked his son and sent him to his room. A little later the Bradys discovered that Tim had torn up three of his picture books while he was in his room.

The Bradys decided to change their approach. Instead of threatening or spanking Tim, they required him to make amends for his destructive behavior. The next time they found Tim tearing a page from a book, they said, "Now you have to fix this book, Tim." They took him by the hand to the tape drawer and helped him tear off the appropriate amount of tape to repair the book.

Tim not only had to fix books, he had to wash walls, scrape crayon off the tiles, and tape cards that he ripped. An interesting thing happened: Tim seldom repeated a destructive behavior once he fixed the damage.

Each time something was damaged, Mr. and Mrs. Brady explained what Tim was allowed to tear and what he was not allowed to tear. The Bradys also encouraged Tim to be as responsible for his possessions as his parents were for theirs. Eventually Tim began to embrace this responsibility. He beamed with pride when his parents praised him for caring for his books, toys, and stuffed animals in a responsible way. And he was quick to make amends whenever he slipped back into his old destructive habits.

As Tim's behavior became less destructive, his parents still didn't expect him to care for his toys as they did their adult toys, but they were careful to model neat behavior so Tim could see that they practiced what they preached about respecting property.

Fighting Cleanup Routines

From a no-more-tears shampoo to disposable diapers, products abound to make bathing, diapering, and shampooing as palatable as possible to preschoolers and their parents. It's expected and even predicted (as these manufacturers know) that preschoolers will find cleanup routines distasteful, so don't feel alone as you persevere with rinsing and soaking. Try to make the cleanup tasks less tedious by diverting your child's attention (sing songs, tell stories) and praising any cooperation (even handing you the soap).

Note: Distinguish between products that irritate your child physically (burns her eyes) as opposed to mentally (all soaps are undesirable) by carefully evaluating her protests. Most parents can tell the difference between distress cries and those that are motivated by anger, frustration, or the desire for attention. Distress cries don't change in tone or duration when parents or other distractions intrude. Other cries generally occur in short bursts interrupted by pauses during which the child listens for a reaction from parents or other caretakers. If necessary, switch from products that irritate your child physically to those that are professionally recommended.

Preventing the Problem

Compromise on cleanup times and places.

Try to make compromises with your child about issues like where you diaper her (on the couch, standing up) or when you wash her hair. Be flexible so your child will not miss a favorite activity just to get her hair washed or miss an episode of a parent-approved television program just to have her diaper changed.

Involve your child in the process.

Help your child play a part in the cleanup or diapering routine. Ask her to bring you things she can carry (according to her age, skill level, and ability to follow directions). Let her pick a favorite toy or towel, for example, to give her a feeling of control over the bathtime routine.

Prepare your child for the cleanup event.

Give your child some warning before a bath, for example, to make the transition from playtime to bathtime less abrupt. Say, "When the timer rings, it will be time for the tub," or, "In a few minutes, we will change your diaper," or, "When we finish this book, it will be time for your bath."

Gather materials before starting.

If your child is too young to help you prepare, make sure you get things ready before beginning the cleanup. This helps avoid unnecessary delays and minimizes frustrations on both ends.

Develop a positive attitude.

Your child will pick up on the dread in your voice if you announce bathtime like it's a prison sentence. If you sound worried or anxious, you're telling her it must be as horrible as she thought. Your attitude is contagious, so make it one that you want imitated.

Solving the Problem

What to Do

Remain calm and ignore the noise.

A calm mood is contagious when dealing with your upset child. If you don't pay attention to the noise, she'll learn that noise has no power over you, which is what she wants when she's resisting your cleaning her up. Say to yourself, "I know my child needs to be diapered. If I don't pay attention to her noise, I'll get this done faster and more effectively."

Have fun in the process.

Distract your child by talking, playing, reciting nursery rhymes, or singing. Say, "Let's sing 'Old MacDonald,'" or, "I'll bet you can't catch this boat and make it dive into the water." Make it a monologue if your child is too young to participate verbally.

Encourage your child to help and shower her with praise.

Ask your child to wash her own tummy, rub on the soap, or open the diaper (if time permits) to give her a feeling of controlling and participating in her personal hygiene. Even the slightest sign of cooperation is a signal for praise. Lather on the words of encouragement. The more your child gets attention for acting as you'd prefer, the more she'll repeat the action to get your strokes. Say, "I really like how you put that shampoo on your hair," or, "That's great the way you're sitting up in the tub," or, "Thanks for lying down so nicely while I diaper you."

Exercise Grandma's Rule.

Let your child know that when she's done something you want her to do (take a bath), she can do something she wants to do (read a story). Say, "When your bath is over, then we'll have a story," or, "When we're finished, then you can play."

Persist in the task at hand.

Despite the kicking, screaming, and yelling, be determined to finish the cleanup process. The more your child sees that yelling isn't going to prevent you from washing away the dirt, the more she'll understand that you'll get the job done faster if she takes the path of least resistance.

Compliment your child when you're done.

Tell your child how delightful she looks and smells. Ask her to go look in the mirror. This will remind her why she needs to have a bath or her diaper changed. Learning to take pride in her appearance will help her make cleanliness a priority.

What Not to Do

Don't demand cooperation.

Just because you demand that your child gets diapered doesn't mean she's going to lie still while you do it. Acting rough and tough only teaches her to be rough and tough, too.

Don't make cleanup painful.

Try to make cleanup as comfortable as possible for your child. Provide towels she can use to wipe her eyes, make the bath water temperature just right, wrap her in a robe after you're done, and so on.

Don't avoid cleanup.

Just because your child resists doesn't mean you should back down. Resistance to cleanup can be overcome by persistence, practice, and patience.

Oceans of Fun

Carol and Phil Porter bathed and shampooed their two-year-old daughter, Lauren, just as they thought most parents they knew did. But they feared something was wrong with Lauren when she screamed and fought her way through these normal cleanup routines. The Porters never experienced this problem with their other daughter, Elizabeth, and none of their friends ever complained about it.

The Porters talked to their pediatrician, who assured them that the soaps, water, and towels were not harmful or irritating. Mr. Porter thought stricter discipline was needed, but they eventually agreed that the best approach was to make cleanup more appetizing to Lauren. The only water-related activity Lauren enjoyed was swimming in the Pacific Ocean during summer vacation. So the Porters decided to call bathtime Oceans of Fun.

That evening they set a timer to ring when it was time to get in the "ocean." During trips to California, they always set a timer to signal when they could go in the real ocean, because Lauren was always begging to get in the water. They hoped this technique would prove helpful at home in Minneapolis, too. "When the timer rings, it will be time to play Oceans of Fun," Mrs. Porter told Lauren. "Let's finish this book while we're waiting."

When the timer rang, Lauren and her mother gathered towels and soap, and Lauren excitedly asked questions about the new game. Lauren smiled with delight as her mom led her to the bathroom where she found the bluest "ocean" she'd ever seen (the result of blue bubble bath) and jaunty boats cruising around a toy ship holding a container of soap (toys Mrs. Porter bought to add to the experience).

Lauren jumped in without a push or an invitation and began playing with the "ocean" toys. Her mother started singing a song about a tugboat, and she gave Lauren a palmful of shampoo to wash her own hair for the first time. The cleanup continued without yelling or screaming—and just a little too much splashing. Mrs. Porter began bathing Lauren in the "ocean" at least once a day, to give her opportunities to learn how to splash less, wash herself more carefully, and enjoy the experience.

Getting into Things

Just getting into first gear in their first year, one-year-olds feel the joy of exploration from their toes to their teeth. They don't automatically know what's off-limits and what isn't, but by two and older they're able to make the distinction once you've set them straight. While restricting the adventures of your little explorers, keep in mind the balance you're trying to strike between letting normal, healthy curiosity be expressed and teaching what behavior is and isn't appropriate.

Preventing the Problem

Childproof your home or apartment.

Keeping doors closed, stairways blocked, cabinets locked, and dangerous areas fenced off will reduce the number of times you have to say no to your child. Children under three years old are busy establishing their independence and making their mark on the world, and they can't understand why they can't go wherever they want. Establishing physical limitations will help you avoid unnecessary confrontations. (See Appendix I.)

Decide what's off-limits.

Decide what your child's boundaries will be and communicate this information early and often. For example, say, "You may play in the living room or in the kitchen, but not in Daddy's office."

Put away valuable items you don't want broken.

A one-, two-, or three-year-old will not understand the difference between an expensive vase and a plastic one. Play it safe by removing valuable items until your little one won't grab for everything despite being told not to.

Teach your child how and when he can go into off-limits areas.

Explain to your child the acceptable ways of playing in off-limits areas. Never allowing him to go into a room or across the street, for example, makes him want to do it even more. Say, "You can go into Mommy's office, but only with Mommy or another adult."

Solving the Problem

What to Do

Use reprimands.

Consistently reprimand your child for a repeated offense, to teach him you mean what you say. Say, "Stop going into that room! I'm sorry you were playing in here. You know this is off-limits. I'd like you to ask Mommy to come with you if you want to go into this room."

Put your child in Time Out.

If your child climbs on the kitchen table repeatedly (and if that's a no-no), reprimand him again and put him in Time Out to reinforce the message.

Compliment your child when he follows the rules.

Tell your child how proud you are of him for remembering not to do certain things. Giving him that compliment will reward his desirable behavior with attention, which will encourage him to do the right thing again. Say, "How nice of you to play in here where you're supposed to," or, "Thanks for not climbing on the coffee table."

Teach your child to touch with his eyes, not his hands.

Tell your child that he may look at a piece of jewelry, for example, with his eyes but not with his hands. This allows him the freedom to explore the item in a limited, controlled way.

What Not to Do

Don't leave guns or knives where children can reach them.

No matter how much safety training children receive, the allure of weapons is too great to resist. Keep all guns locked up, each with its own approved trigger lock, and lock up the ammunition in a separate place that is inaccessible to children. Also, keep *all* knives locked away in a childproof place. It's always better to be safe than sorry.

Don't make no-no's more inviting by getting upset.

If you become angry when your child breaks a rule, he'll see that he can get your attention from misbehavior, and he'll be encouraged to get into trouble more often.

Don't overly punish.

Rather than punishing your child for being naturally curious and getting into things, teach him how to use his curiosity safely—a skill that will serve him well his entire lifetime. Instead of trying to stamp out inappropriate behavior, emphasize the positive.

"Do Not Touch!"

"Curiosity killed the cat" was the line Mrs. Stein remembered her mother saying to her when she climbed on off-limits counters as a youngster. Now she found her fifteen-month-old son, Sam, exploring forbidden lamps and plants. She knew he wasn't being intentionally bad; he was behaving like a normal child. But Mrs. Stein didn't think her reactions to his curiosity seemed normal or showed much self-discipline. "No! Do not touch!" she would shout, slapping her son's hands or spanking him whenever he got into things he knew were no-no's.

Mrs. Stein eventually realized that Sam was only learning to avoid the penalty for getting caught by committing his "crimes" behind her back. So she decided to lock up things she didn't want him to touch, to put breakable items out of reach, and to keep an eye on him as much as possible.

"Touch with your eyes, not your hands," she said to him one particularly active morning when he had started taking everything out of a jewelry box she had forgotten to put on the top shelf. She removed the box and guided her son back to the kitchen where they both had a good time taking the pots and pans out of the cabinet. They also played with the key and lock box and several other toys that provided stimulation for his imagination and curiosity—toys that were appropriate for his age and appropriate for him to take apart and try to destroy.

Once the dangerous and expensive things were removed from Sam's reach and replaced with things he could play with safely, the Steins began having a more pleasant household. Though Mrs. Stein knew she would have to continue monitoring her son's curiosity, she let him have more freedom than before since her house was more childproofed.

One day Sam demonstrated that he was learning the rules when he pointed to a sack of flour he knew was off-limits and said, "No! Mommy's! Do not touch!" To reward his good behavior, Mrs. Stein gave him a sealed box of rice, which he loved to shake like a rattle.

Getting Out of Bed at Night

Children under six years old are famous for piping up with late-night requests for books, kisses, milk, or getting in bed with their parents. Remember that your child's need for sleep is very important. She probably wants those ten books and four drinks to keep you near her, so teach her that going to sleep will bring you back to her bedside faster than demanding attention.

Note: If you're not sure whether your child needs something or merely wants your attention (if she's not talking yet or if she cries out instead of asking for something), go check on her. If all is medically sound, give her a quick kiss and hug (thirty seconds maximum) and make your exit. Tell her firmly and lovingly that it's time for sleep, not play.

Preventing the Problem

Discuss bedtime rules at a nonbedtime time.

Set limits for how many drinks of water or trips to the toilet your child may have at bedtime. Tell her these rules at a neutral time, so she's aware of what you expect her to do when bedtime comes. Say, "You can take two books to bed and have one drink, and I'll tell you two stories before you hit the sack." If your child likes to get in bed with you, decide before she arrives whether your rules allow that. It's up to parents to decide whether they want their children in their bed.

Promise rewards for following the rules.

Make your child aware that following the rules, not breaking them, will bring her rewards. Say, "When you've stayed in your bed all night (if that's your rule), then you may choose your favorite story to read in the morning." Rewards could include special breakfasts, trips to the park, favorite games, or anything else you know is enjoyable for your child.

Reinforce the idea of going back to sleep.

Remind your child of bedtime rules as you put her in bed, to strengthen her memory of previous discussions.

Solving the Problem

What to Do

Follow through with consequences for breaking the rules.

Make breaking the rules more trouble than it's worth. For example, if your child breaks a rule by asking for more than two drinks, go to her bedside and say, "I'm sorry you got out of bed and broke the two-drink rule. Now you must have your door closed, as we said" (if that's what you said you would do if she asked for more drinks of water).

Stand firm with your rules.

Enforce the rule every time your child breaks it, to teach her that you mean what you say. For example, when you put your child back in her bed after she gets in bed with you (in violation of your rule), say, "I'm sorry that you got in bed with us. Remember the rule: Everyone sleeps in her own bed. I love you. See you in the morning."

Follow through with rewards.

Teach your child to trust you by always making good on your promises of rewards for following the rules.

What Not to Do

Don't neglect to enforce the rules.

Once you've set the rules, don't change them unless you discuss this first with your child. Every time you neglect to consistently enforce the rules, your child learns to keep trying to get what she wants, even though you've said no.

Don't give in to noise.

If your child screams because you enforced a rule about going to sleep, remind yourself that she's learning an important health lesson: Nighttime is for sleeping. Time how long your child cries, and chart the progress you're making in getting her not to resist sleep. If you don't respond to the noise, the crying time should gradually decrease and eventually disappear.

Don't use threats and fear.

Threats such as, "If you get out of bed, the lizards will get you," or, "If you do that one more time, I'm going to whip you," will only increase the problem. Unless you back them up, threats are meaningless noises. Fear may keep your child in bed, but the fear may grow until your child becomes afraid of many things.

Don't talk to your child from a distance.
Yelling threats and rules from another room teaches your child to yell, and it tells her you don't care enough to talk to her face to face.

Jennifer's Midnight Ramblings

Two-and-a-half-year-old Jennifer Long had been sleeping through the night since she was six months old. For the past month, however, she had been sleeping only a few hours before waking up her parents with screams of "Mommy! Daddy!" At first, Jennifer's parents would race to see what was wrong with their daughter, only to find her begging for drinks of water one night, an extra hug the next, and bathroom visits on other evenings.

After several weeks of these interruptions, Jennifer's weary parents decided to put a stop to these requests. "If you don't stay in bed, you're going to be punished, young lady," they commanded. Then they returned to their bed, only to hear their daughter padding down the stairs toward their room. They tried spanking Jennifer firmly and telling her to "Get in bed or else!" but their heavy hand seemed to carry little weight.

The Longs kept telling themselves that Jennifer's waking up in the middle of the night was natural; everyone went through periods of shallow and deep sleep. But they also knew that their daughter could choose to go back to sleep instead of calling out to them. They also felt confident in their ability to distinguish between a genuine distress call (an intense and uninterrupted cry) and one that merely sought their attention (short bursts of crying).

To solve the problem, they offered Jennifer more attention for staying in bed. "When you stay in bed without calling out to us," they explained as they tucked her in bed the next night, "you'll have your favorite surprise at breakfast in the morning. When you call out in the middle of the night, we'll close your door, you'll have to stay in bed, and you'll have no surprise." They made sure they stated the new rule in plain terms their daughter could understand.

That night, Jennifer called out for her mother: "I want a drink!" But her mother followed through with her promise to close Jennifer's door and not answer her cries. "I'm sorry you didn't go back to sleep, Jennifer," Mrs. Long said. "Now we'll have to close your door. I'll see you in the morning."

After three nights of closed doors and interrupted sleep for all the Longs, Jennifer learned that calling out did not bring her parents to her bedside and that staying quiet and in bed all night made the promised surprises materialize in the morning. The Longs were finally able to get some uninterrupted sleep, and Jennifer found that their praise for sleeping through the night made her feel grown-up and important—an extra reward.

"Hyper" Activity

"**J**ohn's so hyper!" his grandmother exclaimed after two hours of grueling babysitting with her young grandson. "He wouldn't sit down once...not even to eat!" John's mother had heard the term *hyper* used before to describe her son, and she had even used it herself. But when her mother started complaining about John's behavior, John's mother asked herself, "Is John a normal, busy two-year-old, or is he hyperactive?"

To be clinically diagnosed as hyperactive, a child must fidget frequently, leave his seat, run or climb excessively, have problems playing quietly, be constantly on the go, or be overly talkative. He blurts out answers before the question is completed, has trouble waiting in lines or taking turns, and interrupts or intrudes on others. Because these behaviors often describe the average preschooler, it's very difficult to attach the label of hyperactive to a little whirling dervish. Clinical tests must be done for a proper diagnosis, but even these may not be definitive for preschoolers. If you see four of the above symptoms in your child daily for at least six months, a professional trained in diagnosing hyperactivity can help you understand the difference between a "hyper" active child and a hyperactive child, and he or she can help you manage the behavior of both.

Note: Hyperactivity is considered part of a larger disorder commonly referred to as Attention Deficit Hyperactivity Disorder (ADHD), which comes in three forms: ADHD, predominantly inattentive type; ADHD, predominantly hyperactive/impulsive type; and ADHD, predominantly combined type. All forms of ADHD are difficult to diagnose before children enter formal schooling at about age five, when they're first required to sit and pay attention for longer periods of time, to work while remaining seated, and to memorize material that they'll be tested on later. (See Appendix II.)

Preventing the Problem

Suggest quiet activities.

If your child regularly runs instead of walks and screams instead of talks, introduce calm activities to slow his breakneck speed. For example, play a quiet game, read to him, or have a tiptoe-and-whisper time to teach him that slow and calm is a refreshing change of pace.

Watch your own activity level.

Does hyperactivity run in families? Research has shown that when a parent is diagnosed with hyperactivity, it's highly likely that his or her child will be, too. Look at your own life: Do you ever sit down? Do you talk fast? Is your pace always rushed? If you're a high-energy, always-on-the-go person whose "hyper" activity doesn't get in the way of your success and happiness, then your child may simply have your inborn temperament. Since young children are such great imitators, slowing down your activity level will show your preschooler how to savor the moment.

Avoid "hyper" active TV.

When your child is in constant motion, his entertainment shouldn't be. Wild and crazy television programs model behavior you don't want him to emulate. Turn off the TV to turn off at least one source of noise and "hyper" activity you don't need around the house. Instead, play quiet restful music and encourage TV with a softer tone.

Solving the Problem

What to Do

Practice slowing down.

Give your child opportunities to practice walking—not running—from point A to point B. Say, "Show me how to walk from the kitchen to the family room. I know you can do it. When you walk instead of run, you keep yourself safe." Gradually increase the number of practice walks to a maximum of ten each practice session.

Provide a variety of activities.

Born-to-be-busy children flit like summer houseflies from one activity to another and have trouble staying in one place. Give your "hyper" active child a cafeteria of choices by saying, "You can color on your drawing table, play with clay in the kitchen, or play with your building blocks. I'll set the timer, and you can do one activity until the timer rings. Then you can choose something else if you want." Providing many options lets your child fulfill his need to be busy without driving you to distraction.

Exercise.

Your high-energy child needs constructive outlets in which to satisfy his need to be on the go. Let him run in the park or in your yard whenever you can, or make sure his preschool or daycare provider gives him some running time. Although it may be tempting to sign him up for the neighborhood sports team that all his buddies are on, beware of starting your preschooler too early in sports that can injure his growing body or cause him to burn out before he's ten. Young children need the freedom to rev up their newly charged engines without being corralled in an organized, competitive setting.

Teach relaxation.

When your child learns to relax his body, his motor slows down and he feels less frantic. Help him avoid constantly pushing to do more, faster, sooner by keeping your voice soft and soothing, by rubbing his back, and by talking to him about how calm and relaxed his body feels.

Seek help.

If your child's "hyper" activity endangers his health, alienates others, and jeopardizes his learning, consult a trained professional to determine the cause of his above-average activity level. (See Appendix II.)

What Not to Do

Don't punish.

When your "hyper" active child accidentally collides with your most precious vase, take a deep breath and say, "I'm sorry you chose to run instead of walk. Now you have to practice walking in the house, so I'll know you can do it. Then we'll clean up the mess." In this way, you reach your ultimate goals of teaching your child to walk instead of run, to respect property, and to be responsible for his actions.

Don't ground.

Your busy child needs daily opportunities to play in the great outdoors, so grounding him to the house or his room can cause two problems: (1) His "hyper" activity will swell to explosive levels, and (2) he will only learn to be hyper in the house instead of outside.

Don't rely on medication alone.

Relying on medication alone won't teach your child self-control. Get a thorough evaluation from a professional experienced in assessing "hyper" active children before you decide what behavioral tools and medication are necessary for your child's well-being.

Wild about Ethan

When Jane and Russell Anderson attended Ethan's teacher conference at preschool, they weren't at all surprised at Miss Sharon's comment that their five-year-old son was very active. "He even kept me awake at night when I was pregnant with him, he was so restless and busy," Jane told her. "When Russell is out of town, I let Ethan sleep with me, and it's the same thing. I don't get much sleep because he's so restless. He never walks; he runs. He's just like his dad." Jane put her hand on Russell's knee, which had been in constant motion since he first sat down for the conference.

"Yeah, I was a hyper kid," Russell grinned. "Mom had to go to school lots to bail me out because I was always in trouble for being out of my seat, talking, or doing something stupid. I had to take medication to calm down. Do you think Ethan needs medication?"

"Well, it's not such a big problem in school now, so I don't think medication is called for. But it would be good to keep an eye on him," Miss Sharon told them. "When he's in kindergarten next year, you should work closely with his teacher to see if something more needs to be done. In the meantime, here's a list of things you can do to try to slow him down a bit, as well as the best places you can go for a full evaluation. We believe that children should have a thorough evaluation before starting any kind of medication."

Jane and Russell took the list home and began working with Ethan. Several times a day, they had quiet time during which they read stories or relaxed. At first, Ethan couldn't sit still for more than fifty or sixty seconds, but gradually he began to sit for ten minutes at a time. They also cut out most of the TV Ethan liked to watch and imitate—from wrestling mayhem to martial arts—after his teacher suggested limiting his exposure to such frantic fare. His mom and dad also made a new household rule: "When you're in the house, you must walk. Running is for outside." To teach him the rule, they had Ethan practice navigating the house by walking. This was new to Ethan.

"But what if I'm in a hurry! Why can't I run if I want to?" Ethan whined. Jane smiled inside at Ethan's question. She remembered having to help Russell learn how to slow down after he knocked over a lamp one night trying to get to the kitchen and back before the television commercial was over.

"Because it's against the rule to run in the house," she answered. "Running is for outside where you have lots of room to run and won't bang into the furniture."

Jane also started doing simple relaxation exercises with Ethan at bedtime. She rubbed his back while softly saying, "You're feeling quiet and relaxed. Your feet feel heavy and relaxed, your legs, your tummy, your back, your arms and hands, all feel relaxed and comfortable. Your whole body is relaxed and warm. Your mind is quiet, and you're comfortable and still. Now, Ethan my love, think of being in your bed all quiet and snuggly while you're feeling so calm and quiet."

Ethan gradually became calmer and quieter and somewhat less active. It wasn't always easy for him to keep his body quiet, but he worked at it with his parents and his teacher, which helped prepare him for making a smooth transition to the less active world of the "big school."

Interacting with Strangers

"**D**on't take candy from strangers" is an admonition millions of parents of preschoolers dish out to their young ones. The warning is valid. Children need to learn how to behave with strangers, just as they need to learn how to interact with family, friends, and acquaintances. When you're with your child, minimize her fear of strangers by teaching her how to be friendly to people she doesn't know. At the same time, teach her what to do when approached by a stranger when you're not there. Both you and your child will feel more secure knowing that she understands what to do when you're there and when you're not.

Preventing the Problem

Establish the rules.

Let your child know your rules about interacting with strangers. A basic rule could be, "When I'm with you, you can be friendly and talk to strangers. But when I'm not with you, don't talk to strangers. If a stranger asks you to go with him or tries to give you anything, say, 'No,' and run to the nearest house and ring the doorbell."

Practice following the rules.

Pretend you're a stranger and ask your child to follow your rules concerning strangers. Rehearse several different scenarios, making sure she knows how you want her to respond.

Don't frighten your child.

Instilling fear of strangers only breeds confusion and doesn't teach your child what to do. She needs to know how to think on her feet when strangers invade her privacy. Being fearful will destroy her ability to behave rationally.

Solving the Problem

What to Do

Remind your child of the rule by praising correct behavior.

If your child says hello to a stranger while you're present, show your approval by saying, "I'm so glad you're being friendly. Now tell me the rule about behaving with strangers when I'm not with you." Then praise your child for remembering the rule.

Encourage your child to be friendly.

Friendly children tend to be more readily accepted by others as they go through life, so teaching friendliness is important. However, it's also important to explain to young and older children how to be friendly and keep themselves safe. For example, suggesting that your child say hello to strangers when you're with her encourages her to be friendly. But not allowing her to say anything to strangers when you're not with her helps keeps her safe.

Set stranger boundaries.

It's impossible for children to quickly distinguish between potentially dangerous strangers and ones who are harmless. That's why you have to establish a rule about how to interact with strangers when you're not present. Explain to your child that being friendly with strangers, whether you're there or not, never includes taking offers of candy, gifts, rides, or helping them find lost pets.

What Not to Do

Don't instill fear of people.

To help your child avoid the danger of being molested, teach her your rules about dealing with strangers. However, don't teach her to fear people. Fear only inhibits correct decision making, regardless of age.

Don't worry about your child bothering others by being friendly.

Even if strangers don't acknowledge the greeting, it's good for your child to offer salutations at appropriate times and places.

Keeping Kevin Safe

"How can we teach our three-and-a-half-year-old son to be friendly, yet keep him safe when we're not around?" This was the challenge Mr. and Mrs. Docking faced in trying to solve the problem of their overly friendly son, Kevin. *"Some day someone might take advantage of your friendliness,"* they explained to Kevin, *"so do not talk to strangers."*

Kevin followed their orders so intently that he became terrified of strangers and began to throw tantrums every time his parents took him to the shopping center or grocery store. He didn't want to see strangers, he explained to his mother, because they were so mean and dangerous that he couldn't even say hello to them.

The Dockings were frustrated to see their well-intentioned instructions backfire this way. They finally realized that Kevin didn't understand the difference between saying hello, which they wanted to encourage when they were with him, and saying hello or going with strangers or taking things from them, which they wanted to prevent when they weren't with him. Kevin didn't understand because the Dockings had not given him the chance to understand.

"Strangers may hurt you if you go places with them or take things from them," Mrs. Docking told her son. *"The new rule is that you can talk to anyone you want when I'm with you. But if I'm not with you and someone offers you something or wants you to go somewhere with him, ignore the person and go to the nearest house or nearest adult in a store."* The Dockings practiced this rule by taking Kevin to a shopping center and rehearsing his actions while his mother played the "stranger."

Mrs. Docking reminded her son of the rule on a weekly basis, until it became a habit for him. To reinforce the lesson, Mrs. Docking practiced saying hello to others, too. Kevin noticed this and praised her for it, just as she had praised him for following the rule.

The Dockings' concern for Kevin's safety never completely disappeared. They had Kevin practice stranger safety from time to time, to convince themselves that he understood and remembered this potentially life-saving behavior.

Interrupting

Because a preschooler's most priceless possession is his parents' attention, he'll try anything to get it back when the telephone, doorbell, or another person takes it away. Limit the tricks your child tries to play to get your undivided attention by providing him with special playthings reserved for those times when you're chatting with the competition. This will keep your child busy without you, while you're busy without him.

Preventing the Problem

Limit the length of your conversations.

Your child has a limited ability to delay gratification, so keep your conversations short while your child is nearby, unoccupied, and wanting your attention.

Practice "play" telephone.

Teach your child what you mean by *not interrupting* by practicing with two play phones—one for you and one for him. Tell him, "This is how I talk on the phone, and this is how you play while I'm on the phone." Then let your child pretend to talk on the phone while you play without interrupting him. This shows him what he can do instead of interrupting you.

Set up activities for telephone playtime.

Gather special toys and materials in a drawer near the phone. (Let children over two years old choose their materials). Have your child play with those toys while you're on the phone. To further reduce the likelihood of his interrupting you, periodically give him attention by smiling and telling him how nicely he's playing. Some materials require adult supervision (fingerpaints, watercolors, Play-Doh, shaving cream, and magic markers, for example), so make them available to your preschooler only when you're able to watch him carefully. Make sure the phone toys match your child's skill level, to reduce the possibility of his needing to interrupt you for help.

Solving the Problem

What to Do

Praise nice playing and not interrupting.

If your child is getting attention (smiles, praise, and so on) for playing and not interrupting, he'll be less inclined to barge in on your conversation. Excuse yourself momentarily from your conversation and say to your child, "Thanks for playing so nicely with your toys. I'm so proud of you for having fun on your own."

Whenever possible, involve your child in your conversation.

When a friend visits, try to include your child in your conversation. This will reduce the possibility of his interrupting you to get attention.

What Not to Do

Don't get angry and yell at your child for interrupting.

Yelling at your child about any behavior only encourages him to yell.

Don't interrupt people, especially your child.

Even if your child is a constant chatterbox, show him you practice what you preach by not interrupting him while he's talking.

Use Grandma's Rule.

Use a timer to let your child know that you'll soon be all his again. He can earn your attention and have fun at the same time. Tell him, "When you've played with your toys for two minutes and the timer rings, I'll be through talking on the phone and I'll play with you."

Reprimand and use Time Out.

Use a reprimand such as, "Stop interrupting. I cannot talk to my friend while I'm being interrupted. Instead of interrupting, please play with your cars." If your child continues to interrupt, use Time Out to remove him from the possibility of getting attention for interrupting. Say, "I'm sorry that you're continuing to interrupt. Time out."

"Not Now, Lin!"

Whenever Mrs. Wilkens talked on the phone, her three-year-old daughter, Lin, interrupted the conversation with requests for drinks of apple juice or toys from the "high place." She also asked questions like, "Where are we going today?" Although Mrs. Wilkens wanted to answer, she tried to explain calmly at each interruption, "Sweetheart, Mommy is on the phone. Please don't interrupt." But Lin continued to interrupt.

So one day Mrs. Wilkens started screaming, "Don't interrupt me! You're a bad girl!" She also gave her daughter a swift swat on the bottom to shut her up. Not only did the swat not shut Lin up, it angered her into crying and screaming so loudly that her mother couldn't continue her conversation. The more her mother screamed, the more Lin interrupted—a cause-and-effect situation that Mrs. Wilkens finally understood and decided to reverse. She would now give her daughter attention for not interrupting instead of interrupting.

The next morning, Sally called Mrs. Wilkens for their regular Monday morning chat. But Mrs. Wilkens told her that she couldn't talk because she was playing with the children. As she was explaining this to her friend, she noticed how Lin had begun playing with the toys Mrs. Wilkens had gathered around the phone. "Thanks for not interrupting!" she said to Lin, giving her a big hug.

When she got off the phone, Mrs. Wilkens again praised Lin, "Thanks for not interrupting me while I told Sally about our dinner tonight. She wanted a recipe for meat loaf. These markers are here for you to play with, if you want, while I talk on the phone." The toys were especially fascinating to Lin because they were called "telephone" toys—ones she was allowed to play with only when her mother was on the phone.

The next time the phone rang, both Lin and her mother smiled with anticipation. "Lin, the phone is ringing. Let's play with the telephone toys." Lin ran to get the markers. While talking on the phone, Mrs. Wilkens watched Lin carefully and encouraged her uninterruptive behavior with an occasional, "Nice playing."

Jealousy

Toddlers and preschoolers believe they should get undivided attention whenever they order it because they live at the center of their universe. This self-centered view of life is the source of sibling rivalry and jealousy. When the attention they demand isn't there because it's being given to a new baby, another sibling, or even a spouse, preschoolers often morph into green-eyed monsters. Smitten with jealousy, they sulk, sabotage, scream, or solicit more attention by hitting their siblings, breaking toys, throwing tantrums, and so on. Justified or not, your child's jealousy can tear your heart out. Interpret her jealous behavior as a teachable moment by giving her both the attention she needs and the opportunity to be helpful. (See "Sibling Rivalry" on pages 118–121 for additional insights into problems involving jealousy.)

Preventing the Problem

Keep your child involved.

While you're changing the baby, for example, enlist your child's help by asking her to get a new diaper, hold the lotion, or entertain the baby. If your preschooler becomes jealous while you're hugging your hubby, a bigger hug to include her can put the wind back into her sails.

Praise sharing.

When your child accepts your attention being directed elsewhere, point out her willingness to share by saying, "That was so nice of you to share me with the baby. Thanks for being so generous."

Help your child feel special.

To keep the green-eyed monster at bay, allow an older sibling to help open the baby's gifts and show them to the baby. Encouraging friends and relatives to bring gifts for both children helps keep the older child feeling special.

Solving the Problem

What to Do

Show empathy.

When jealousy flares, tell your child you understand how she feels by saying, "I know you don't like it when I have to take care of the baby, but I think you can handle it. After you play with your building blocks until I'm through, then I'll play with you."

Provide alternative activities.

Understand that your child gets jealous because she feels left-out when you and your spouse want some time together. Give your child something constructive to do until you're ready to give her your undivided attention. Say, "Daddy and I want to talk for a while. You can play with your toys until the timer rings. Then you can talk to me if you want."

Monitor your time.

To a child, love is spelled T-I-M-E. Consider how much time you spend with your child reading stories, answering questions, sharing meals, playing games, and so on. When your child feels secure in your love, her jealousy meter stays low because she knows she's your number one priority. Tell her "I love you" many times each day. Strengthen your bond with each of your children by making special play dates for just the two of you so each child feels valued and important.

Turn jealousy into helpfulness.

A young child wants her world to exist for her alone, but she also wants to be independent. She needs to learn that independence comes at a price: She has to give up having her parents' undivided attention to gain a sense of control and self-determination. By teaching toddlers and preschoolers to be helpful toward siblings and others when feeling left-out and jealous, you're helping them turn negative behavior into something positive and praiseworthy. Say, "I know you want me to play with you now, but first I have to take your brother to soccer practice. Come help me put the oranges in the sack so the boys will have a treat. You can have one, too."

What Not to Do

Don't compare your child to siblings or others.

Saying, "I wish you could be as helpful as your little brother," or, "Why can't you be as sweet as your big sister?" only tells your child that she's not living up to who you want her to be. To children, that translates into not being as lovable as other family members, which is a sure-fire way to stir up the green-eyed monster.

Don't punish.

When your child gets out of sorts because she wants your undivided attention, punishing her for being upset will only increase her sense of alienation. Instead, show her how she can better cope with not getting the attention she wants when she wants it. Say, "I'm sorry you're so upset because I can't play right now. Let's make a deal. I'll play with your baby sister for a while, and when the timer rings, I'll read your book to you. Next time, we'll switch, and you can go first."

Green-Eyed Jana

Jana Goodman was really excited when she learned that she was going to have a baby brother or sister. She loved the idea of having a new playmate, which seemed to her like a new toy. Her parents, Sam and Christine Goodman, were convinced that Jana wouldn't have any problems accepting the new baby. But were they in for a surprise!

Everything went well the first few days after Baby Jay was brought home, because Grammy was there and Jana got lots of attention. Jana told her mom and dad that she thought Baby Jay looked funny, didn't smell very good sometimes, and wasn't able to play with her like she wanted. But she reassured her mom by saying, "I guess it's okay if he stays. Let's keep him for a while."

However, when Grammy left to go back home—a thousand miles away—Jana realized that her mom had to spend way too much time taking care of Baby Jay. Jana decided she needed to reassert herself as the "number one kid" in her house.

She tried whining for a while, but that didn't make her mom leave Baby Jay and come play with her. Then she tried sulking, but nobody seemed to pay any attention to that, either. So she started refusing to do what her mom and dad asked, like putting away her toys or brushing her teeth. Her mom was exasperated by this change of attitude and said, "Jana, what's gotten into you? It's Time Out for you, little missy."

When Sam came home that evening and heard what Jana had done, his first response was, "Oh yes, the green-eyed monster has come to visit. Your mother warned us this might happen."

So the Goodmans developed a plan to involve Jana in caring for Baby Jay. She became Mommy's Little Helper and was eager to assist when Baby Jay was being changed or fed. She even held the storybook so Christine could read to her while feeding Baby Jay. When Grammy came to visit, she brought Jana a little gift as well as one for Baby Jay. Jana got to open Baby Jay's gift so she could show him what Grammy brought. Grammy also spent plenty of time with Jana so she didn't feel so left-out when Grammy was holding Baby Jay.

Like a miracle, green-eyed Jana became a much more pleasant child to have around. The Goodmans knew that their empathy for Jana helped her accept the new family member and the important responsibility of being a big sister.

Lying

Toddlers and preschoolers live in an interesting world where fantasy and reality mix. They enjoy cartoons, pretend play, Santa Claus, wicked witches, flying capes, make-believe on demand, and so on. Their storytelling often reveals hidden fears. For example, "Mommy, there's a monster in my room! Come save me!" may be your child's way of telling you he's afraid of the dark. Toddlers and preschoolers can be convinced of almost anything. If they want to believe something badly enough, they can convince themselves of the truth in even the biggest lie.

Lying signals another step toward independence, as fledglings stretch their wings and push away from parental control. So what's a parent to do? Your job is to understand the flavor of the lie and sell your child on the benefits of telling the truth. Knowing that the truth is important to you will make being honest more important to your child.

Preventing the Problem

Reinforce telling the truth.

Offer praise when you know you're hearing the truth, whether it's about something bad that happened or something good. This helps the under-six set begin to understand the difference between what's true and what's not.

Tell the truth.

When your preschooler asks for a cookie right before dinner, you might be tempted to say, "We don't have any cookies," instead of telling him the truth, which is, "I don't want you to eat a cookie before dinner." By lying to him, you're telling him that it's okay to lie when he wants to get out of doing something unpleasant. He knows where the cookies are, so don't pretend he doesn't. Say, "I know you want a cookie now, but when you've eaten your dinner, you can pick one out yourself."

Learn the flavors of lying.

Lying comes in a variety of flavors. Plain old vanilla is the one we all know so well: lying to stay out of trouble. "I didn't take the last cookie" is a good example. A more pungent flavor is lying to get out of doing something you don't want to do. For example, your child might say, "Sure,

Mommy, I brushed my teeth," when he hasn't. And then there's the ever popular, extrasmooth lying that gets whipped up when children try to impress others with comments like, "I have *three* horses that I get to ride every day. So there!"

Be empathetic.

Understand the flavor of lying your child is using and respond accordingly. For example, when your child tells you that he didn't mark his bedroom wall with crayons even though you know he did, tell him, "I understand that you don't want to be punished, but I'm more disappointed that you chose to lie rather than tell the truth. You can always tell me the truth so we can fix the problem together." Your child will feel more comfortable facing the music and telling the truth when he knows you'll be sensitive to his feelings.

Look for honesty.

Look for people and events that demonstrate honesty and truth. Point these out to your preschooler to reinforce your message that being honest is important.

Solving the Problem

What to Do

Show how lying hurts.

When your child is caught in a lie, explain to him how it hurts him as well as you. "I'm sorry you chose not to tell the truth. It makes me feel sad that I can't trust what you say. Let's work on telling the truth so I can believe what you tell me is true."

Explain the difference between lying and telling the truth.

Preschoolers don't always know that what they're saying is a lie because it might seem like the truth to them. Help your child understand the difference between reality and fantasy by saying, "I know you want your friend to like you, but telling him that you have 101 dalmatians living at your house isn't truthful. The truth is that you'd *like* to have all those dogs, but you only have one dog named Molly. She's a really nice dog, and you love her a lot."

Help your child accept responsibility.

When you send your son to do a chore such as putting the toys away in his room, he might lie to get out of doing the job by telling you that he already did it. Say, "I'm so glad you did what I asked. I'll go see what a great job you did." If your son says, "Oh no, Mommy, not yet," you can be reasonably sure he's avoided his responsibility. Check it out! If you discover that he lied, say, "I'm sorry you chose to lie about doing what I asked. I know you didn't want to put all those toys away and didn't want me to be disappointed, but doing what I ask and telling the truth are important. Now let's go get the job done. I'll watch while you pick up."

Practice telling the truth.

When your child lies to you, he's letting you know he needs practice telling the truth. Say, "I'm sorry you didn't tell me the truth when I asked you if you had turned off the TV. Let's practice telling the truth. I want you to say, 'Yes, Mommy, I'll turn off the TV when this show is over.' Now let's try it."

Play make-believe with your child.

To help your child understand the difference between truth and fiction, set aside time for him to make up stories. Then contrast this make-believe time with truth time in which he's asked to tell the truth about what happened. When your child tells you something you know isn't true, say, "That's an interesting make-believe story you just told me. Now tell me a true story about what really happened."

What Not to Do

Don't test your child's honesty.

If you know your child has done something wrong, asking him a question to which you already know the answer forces him into a dilemma: tell the truth and get punished, or lie and maybe get away with it. Don't make him choose.

Don't punish.

When you catch your child telling a lie in order to stay out of trouble, don't punish him for doing so. Instead, teach him how to accept responsibility for making a mistake and to fix the problem it caused. For example, say, "I'm sorry the wall has marks on it. Now we're going to have to learn about taking care of walls. Let's get the cleaning stuff and start cleaning. I'll get the cleaner while you get the paper towels. See? Telling me the truth lets us fix the problem."

Don't lie.

Avoid exaggerating or making up stories to impress people, avoid consequences, or get out of doing what you don't want to do.

Don't overreact.

Even if you've said a hundred times that you can't stand a liar, going ballistic when your child lies only forces him to avoid telling the truth in order to keep you from being mad.

Don't label your child a "liar."

Don't make lying a self-fulfilling prophecy. A child who's called a "liar" will believe that what he does is what he is. Your child isn't what he does. You might not love his behavior, but you'll always love him unconditionally.

Don't take lying personally.

Little Danny isn't telling you an exaggerated version of his morning at daycare just to make you crazy. He may actually believe that the classroom's pet snake got out of its cage because he was so scared that it would. Listen to his story and tell him, "That's an interesting story, sweetheart. I'm sure having the snake loose in the room would be really scary. Do you want me to talk to Miss Laura about keeping the snake safely locked up in its cage?"

"Don't You Lie to Me!"

Although Larry Kirk had just turned four years old, his parents had already tagged him as a "liar." He'd come home from preschool and tell Julie, his mother, the most fantastic stories about how somebody broke into his school and held everyone hostage, or how his teacher had been told she couldn't work there anymore, or how his friend, Adam, had brought his pony to school. Every day it was something new, and Julie was becoming afraid that Larry's fantasies were getting out of hand.

Lawrence, Larry's dad, had also heard Larry's tall tales. He had recently confronted his son about some juice that had been spilled in the kitchen, and the answer he got astonished him. Larry tried to convince his dad that someone broke into the house to steal stuff and must have spilled the juice on the floor. "But son, it's the same grape juice that you have in your cup right now. How do you explain that? Now don't you lie to me!" When Larry didn't have an answer, he was put in Time Out.

Julie and Lawrence realized that this consequence would not teach their son to tell the truth, because the more they put him in Time Out, the more he lied. He even tried to lie his way out of Time Out.

Julie and Lawrence loved their son and needed to help him understand that they would love him no matter what happened. They also knew that their son didn't have to lie to impress them or to stay out of trouble, but they weren't sure if he knew that. When they thought about how the world must seem to little children—a confusing blend of fantasy and reality—the Kirks understood that they could help their son by teaching him the difference between truth and fiction.

"Tell me about school today," Julie said when Larry got into the car after preschool the next day.

"Well, today was real neat because the football team that plays in the stadium came and showed us how to play football, but Josh got hurt and they had to take him to the hospital in an ambulance..." Larry began, but Julie stopped him.

"Wow!" she exclaimed. "That must have been exciting. Is this what you wanted to happen today at school, or did this really happen?"

"Well..." Larry answered, "I wished it happened. Then school would have been more exciting."

"Larry, your story was very interesting, but I really want to know the truth. You don't have to make up things about school so I'll think your day was exciting. You can tell me about the games you played, who sat next to you at snack time, what Miss Sharon talked about, and all sorts of things that I'd like to hear about. I have an idea. You like to make up stories, so let's have story time when you can make up stories, and then let's have truth time when you can report what actually happened during your day."

Larry got into the habit of saying, "Story time, Mom." Then he'd launch into a fantastic tale about his day at school, and they'd both laugh. Julie would rave about how much she enjoyed story time.

"Now it's truth time, Larry," his mom would say, and he'd report on the more mundane events of the day. Julie would tell Larry how much she loved his truth-time tales, too. Lawrence and Julie accomplished two goals: They taught their son lessons in honesty, and they taught him how important telling the truth was to them.

Messiness

Little people make big messes, and unfortunately for orderly parents, small children are almost always oblivious to their self-made clutter. Knowing that your child isn't deliberately messy but simply unaware of the need to clean up after herself, teach her (the younger the better) that messes don't disappear magically—the mess maker (with helpers) cleans them up. Share this fact of life with your child, but don't expect perfection in her following the rule. Encourage rather than demand neatness by praising the slightest attempt your child makes at playing the cleanup game.

Preventing the Problem

Clean as you go.

Show your child how to put away her toys immediately after she's done playing, to limit clutter as she bounces from plaything to plaything. Help her pick up the picking-up habit early in life, to encourage her to be a neater child and, later, a more organized adult.

Show her how to clean up her mess.

Provide appropriately sized boxes and cans in which your child can store her toys and other playthings. Show her how to fit her things inside the containers and where they go when they're filled. This way she'll know exactly what you mean when you ask her to put something away or clean something up.

Be as specific as you can.

Instead of asking your child to clean up her room, tell her exactly what you'd like her to do. For example, say, "Let's put the pegs in the bucket and the blocks in the box." Make it as simple as possible for your child to follow your instructions.

Provide adequate cleanup supplies.

Don't expect your child to know what to use to clean up her mess by herself. For example, give her the right cloth to wash off the table. Make sure to praise all her cleanup efforts after you've given her the tools of the trade.

Confine messy activities to a safe place.

Avoid potential catastrophes by letting your child play with messy materials (fingerpaints, clay, markers, crayons, and so on) in appropriate places. Don't expect her to know not to destroy the living-room carpet when you've let her fingerpaint in there.

Solving the Problem

What to Do

Use Grandma's Rule.

If your child refuses to clean up a mess she's made, make her fun dependent on doing the job you've requested. For example, say, "Yes, I know you don't want to pick up your blocks. But when you've picked them up, then you may go outside to play." Remember that a child one year old or older can help clean up in small ways. She needs to try her best at whatever level she can, slowly building up to more difficult tasks.

Work together.

Sometimes the cleanup job is too big for a young child's muscles or hands. Join in the work to encourage sharing and cooperation—two lessons you want your child to learn as a preschooler. Seeing Mom or Dad clean up makes the activity that much more inviting.

Play Beat-the-Clock.

When your child is trying to beat the timer, picking up toys is a fun game instead of an arduous task. Join in the fun by saying, "When you've picked up the toys before the timer rings, you can take out another toy." When your child is successful at beating the clock, praise her accomplishment and follow through on your promise.

Praise your child's cleanup effort.

Encourage your child to clean up after herself by using a powerful motivator—praise! Comment on the great job she's doing putting away her crayons, for example. Say, "I'm really glad you put that red crayon in the basket. Thanks for helping clean up your room."

What Not to Do

Don't expect perfection.

Your child hasn't had much time to practice cleaning up after herself, so don't expect her job to be perfect. The fact that she's trying means she's learning how to do it. She'll improve over time.

Don't punish messiness.

Your child cannot yet understand the value of neatness and doesn't have the physical maturity to stay tidy, so punishing her for being messy will not teach her the cleanup skills she needs to learn.

Don't expect preschoolers to dress themselves for a mess.

Your child doesn't understand the value of nice clothing, so provide her with old clothes (and put them on inside out, if you want) before allowing her to play with messy materials.

Multiple Messes

As parents, John and Mandy Wareman were getting used to everything but the messes their five-year-old twins, Leah and Hannah, made almost daily. "Good children always put away their toys," Mrs. Wareman told them, trying to convince the girls not to leave their toys in the living room when they were done playing. When that didn't work, she began spanking her daughters and putting them in their rooms when they didn't clean up their mess. But that punishment seemed to punish only her, because the girls created additional messes while in their rooms.

Mrs. Wareman finally saw a way to solve the problem when she realized how much her children liked to play outside on their new swing set. She decided to turn that activity into a privilege that had to be earned. One day the girls wanted to go outside instead of cleaning up the pegs and the kitchen set they had been playing with. Mrs. Wareman said, "Here's the new rule, girls. I know you want to go outside, but when you've picked up your kitchen set, Leah, and your pegs, Hannah, then you can play on the swing set. I will help."

The two girls looked at each other. They didn't want to pick up their toys, but they really wanted to play on the swing set. Mrs. Wareman began helping put the pegs in the jar to make sure that Hannah knew what clean up the pegs meant. Mrs. Wareman also opened up the bag so Leah could deposit the kitchen utensils in their proper place, leaving no doubt about what cleaning up the kitchen set *meant.*

As the girls began cleaning up, Mrs. Wareman let them know how happy she was with their efforts. "Thanks for cleaning up. You're doing a great job filling that jar with pegs. I sure like the way that kitchen set fits into that tiny bag." She hugged each girl with genuine pride, and soon both children spilled out the door, leaving their mother to fix lunch instead of clean up after them.

For many weeks, the girls needed to be offered rewards for cleaning up, but they finally learned that putting away one toy before taking out another made the cleanup process quicker and also brought great compliments from Mom.

Name-Calling

Blossoming preschool linguists test the power of name-calling to let the world know that they're the boss and can talk like it. By calling people names, your child is testing the strength of words as well as the reactions they get. If you react calmly when he calls you a name, you'll teach him that name-calling will not achieve his desired effect. Explain that he should also react calmly when he's called a name. He'll realize that the name-calling game isn't much fun when played by only one.

Preventing the Problem

Watch your nicknames.
Avoid calling your child nicknames you wouldn't want him to call someone else. There's a big difference between "You little devil" and "You little doll."

Teach your child to respond calmly to name-calling.
Suggest appropriate ways for your child to react when he's the victim of name-calling. Encourage him to avoid getting angry. Say, "When your friend calls you a bad name, tell him calmly that you can't play with him when he calls you names."

Decide what's a bad name and what isn't.
Make sure you've educated your child about "illegal" names before expecting him to know what they are.

Solving the Problem

What to Do

Put your child in Time Out.
For example, say, "When you do things that aren't acceptable, you lose your chances for playing. I'm sorry you called your sister a bad name. Time out."

Wear out the name.
For some preschoolers, repeating a name takes away its power. Put your child in a chair and have him repeat the word without stopping (one

minute for each year of age). If he refuses to do so (many preschoolers do), simply have him sit there until he starts, no matter how long it takes. When he's done, focus on teaching him appropriate things to say.

Notice nice talk.

Praise your child when he's using appropriate language instead of name-calling, to help him distinguish between what's acceptable and what's not.

Be consistent.

Every time your child is the name-caller, use the same response to teach him that name-calling is never acceptable. Say, "I'm sorry you called your friend a name. Now you'll have to go to Time Out," or, "Now you must wear out the word."

What Not to Do

Don't be a name-caller.

Because being called names is so irritating, it's easy to shout back at your child the same hurtful words he says to you. Saying something like, "You dummy! You should know better than to call people names," gives your preschooler permission to use the names you used. Instead, channel your anger into an explanation of how and why you feel upset. Your child will learn when his words make you unhappy and how you'd like him to behave when he feels like name-calling.

Don't use severe punishment for name-calling.

If you severely punish your child for name-calling, he'll only learn to avoid the behavior when you're within earshot. Instead of learning that name-calling is wrong, he'll learn that he needs to avoid getting caught. Punished behavior does not go away; it just goes out of sight.

"That's Not Nice!"

Max and Suzanne Glass were shocked when they first heard their precious four-year-old daughter, Sarah, call her friends "dummy," "jerk," and "dog poo poo." They had never used these words around the house, so they couldn't understand where Sarah had picked them up, and they didn't know what to do about it.

"Don't call people names, Sarah! That's not nice!" they would say every time their daughter used an offending word, but this had little effect. In fact,

Sarah soon began calling her parents names, which caused them to spank her. But even this didn't stop the name-calling.

Finally, Mrs. Glass tried a different strategy. She began to supervise her daughter's play more closely, to notice when Sarah played well with others and when she didn't. "How nicely you girls are getting along," Mrs. Glass pointed out when Sarah and her cousin, Maria, were dressing their baby dolls. But when Maria tried to take Sarah's doll for a ride in the blue car, Sarah yelled, "You dummy, Maria, you know that's my car."

Mrs. Glass immediately separated the girls. "I'm sorry you called your cousin a 'dummy,'" she told Sarah. "Time out." After four minutes in the Time Out chair, Sarah learned that her mother meant business. Playtime would be halted and Sarah would be put in Time Out if she called anyone names. Sarah started to learn that name-calling was hurtful, and the behavior began to disappear.

Not Following Directions

Preschoolers love to test whether their parents' warnings will be enforced, how far rules can be stretched, and how closely directions must be followed. Give your child consistent results for her research on the adult world. Prove to your child that you mean what you say so she'll feel more secure about what she can expect from other adults. Your making and enforcing rules may seem dictatorial to your child, but despite her protests she will feel more secure knowing that limits are set and rules are defined as she moves from a little to a big person's world.

Preventing the Problem

Learn how many directions your child can follow at once.

Your preschooler will only be able to remember and follow a certain number of directions, depending on her developmental stage. To find out your child's limit, give one simple direction, then two, then three. For example, for three directions say, "Please pick up the book, put it on the table, and come sit by me." If all three are followed in the proper order, you'll know your child can remember three directions. Identify her limit and wait until she's older before giving her more complicated directions.

Let your preschooler do as many things by herself as possible.

Because she wants to follow the beat of her own drum and have total control over her life, your preschooler will fight for the chance to make choices. Whenever possible, give her the opportunity to develop her decision-making skills and increase her self-confidence. The more control she feels she has, the less likely she'll be to reject taking directions from someone else.

Avoid unnecessary rules.

Analyze a rule's importance before you etch it in stone. Your preschooler needs as much freedom as possible to develop her independence.

Solving the Problem

What to Do

Give simple, clear directions.

Be as specific as possible about what you want your child to do, to make it easier for her to follow your directions. Make suggestions but try not to criticize what she's done. For example, say, "Please pick up your toys now and put them in the box," rather than, "Why don't you ever remember to pick up your toys and put them away on your own?"

Praise following directions.

Reward your child for following your directions by praising her job well done. You can also show her how to appreciate someone's effort by saying, "Thank you for doing what I asked you to do."

Use countdown.

Make the rule that your child must start a task by the count of five, for example, to ease her into the idea of leaving her fun for something you want her to do. Say, "Please pick up your toys now. Five-four-three-two-one." Thank her for starting to clean up so quickly, if she does.

Praise your child's progress.

Be a cheerleader as your child takes steps toward completing your requested task. For example, say, "That's great the way you're getting up and starting to put those toys away."

Use Grandma's Rule.

Children are more likely to follow directions when they know they can do what they want to do after a task is completed. For example, say, "When you've picked up the books, you may turn on the television," or, "When you've washed your hands, we will have lunch."

Practice following directions.

If your child is not following your directions, find out whether she's unable or unwilling by walking her through the task. Guide her manually and praise her progress along the way. If you discover she can do the task but simply refuses to do so, say, "I'm sorry you aren't following directions. Now we have to practice." Practice five times, then give her the opportunity to follow the directions on her own. If she still refuses, say, "It looks like we need more practice. When you finish practicing, then you may play with your toys."

What Not to Do

Don't back down if your child resists.

Say to yourself, "I know my child doesn't want to do as I say, but I'm more experienced and know what's best for her. I need to teach her by giving her clear directions so she can eventually do things herself."

Don't punish your child for not following directions.

Teaching your child how to do something, instead of punishing her for not doing it, avoids damaging her self-esteem and doesn't put attention on her failure to follow directions.

"Do What You're Told!"

Four-and-a-half-year-old Eric Jackson knew his alphabet and his numbers, and he was even starting to sound out words in his favorite books. The one thing he couldn't do was the one thing his mother wanted most: follow her directions.

On a daily basis, Eric's mother would give him simple directions like, "Eric, please pick up your toys and then put your dirty clothes in the hamper," or, "Come sit here on the couch and put on your boots." Eric would get about halfway through the first task, then he'd lose track of what he was supposed to be doing and wander off to investigate a toy truck or to see what his brother was doing.

"How many times do I have to tell you what to do?" his frustrated mother would yell. "You never listen to me! You never understand what I tell you!" she would continue, giving him a swift spanking for not complying with her wishes.

This continued until one day Eric shouted back, "I can't do what you want!" His mother actually heard what he said and took it seriously. She decided to try limiting her directions to one simple command, to see if Eric could do that.

"Eric, please bring me your boots," she asked simply. Eric marched right over to his blue and white boots and brought them to his mother, who clapped her hands with delight. "Thanks so much for doing what I asked!" A while later, she asked Eric to go get his coat on. When Eric fulfilled her request, she again followed up with praise for his effort.

Eric's mother was delighted that she could stop threatening and screaming at her son. She realized that listening to Eric's feelings was crucial to their getting along. She slowly increased the number of directions she gave her son, waiting until he was able to do two at a time before giving him three at a time. Her clear language and use of Grandma's Rule helped her win the war against not following directions.

Not Sharing

Mine is the buzzword preschoolers use to remind each other (and adults) of their territorial rights. Despite the wars this four-letter word incites in households with children under five years old, possessiveness will unfortunately not disappear until children are developmentally ready to let it go (between three and four years old). Help lay the groundwork for peace by consistently teaching your preschooler the give-and-take rules of the world. Enforce these sharing rules at home, but be patient. Don't expect them to be righteously followed until you see your child sharing without your intervention—the glorious sign that he's ready to broaden his boundaries.

Preventing the Problem

Make sure some toys belong strictly to your child.

Before preschoolers can let go of the word *mine* and all the things attached to it, they must be given the chance to possess things. Put away your child's favorite toys or blankets when visitors come over to play so he won't be forced to share them.

Point out how you and your friends share.

Show your child that he isn't the only one in the world expected to share his things. Give examples at neutral (nonsharing) times of how you and your friends share things. Say, "Mary borrowed my cookbook today," or, "Charlie borrowed my lawnmower."

Point out what sharing means and how much you like it.

Tell your child how nicely he's sharing whenever he's allowing another person to hold or play with his toys. For example, say, "I like the way you're sharing by letting your friend have that toy for a minute."

Put labels on similar toys (for twins or children close in age).

Make sure you don't confuse your son's teddy bear with his sister's or brother's, if they're the same. Label each one with a nametag or piece of thread to help your children feel confident in their ownership.

Set up sharing rules.

Before friends come over to play, let your child know what's expected of him at group sharing times. For example, say, "If you put a toy down, anyone may play with it. If you have it in your hands, you may keep it."

Understand that your child may share better at a friend's house.

Your child may be less aggressive about ownership when he's not defending his own territory.

Remember that sharing is a developmental task.

Learning to share is an accomplishment that cannot be rushed. Usually at three to four years of age, your child will begin sharing things without being reminded.

Solving the Problem

What to Do

Supervise one- and two-year-olds' play.

Because children younger than three years old cannot be expected to share, stay close by while they're playing, to help resolve sharing conflicts they're too young to handle without assistance.

Set the timer.

When two children are calling a toy "mine," show how the give-and-take of sharing works. Tell one child that you'll be setting the timer, and when the timer rings, the other child can have the toy. Keep using the timer until they've grown tired of the toy.

Put toys in Time Out.

If a toy is creating a problem because one child won't share, put the toy in Time Out to remove it from the situation. If the toy is out of reach, it can't cause any trouble. Say, "This toy is causing a problem. It must go into Time Out." If the children keep fighting over the toy after it's been brought out, keep removing it to make the point that not sharing a toy means no one gets to play with it.

What Not to Do

Don't get upset.

Remember that your child will learn the rule about sharing when he's developmentally ready, not when you force him to do so. When you see your child sharing, you'll know he's ready!

Don't punish for occasionally not sharing.

If your child occasionally has trouble sharing, remove the offending toy rather than punish your child. This puts the blame on the toy, not the child.

Learning to Share

Three-year-old Cody Smith knew what the word sharing *meant; it meant that he couldn't sit and hold as many toys as he wanted when his friend, Jim, came over to play. "You* must *share!" Cody's mother told her son after another day of Cody clutching his toys and saying "Mine" whenever his mother said, "Now, Cody, let's share."*

One day Mrs. Smith screamed, "I'm going to give all your toys to poor children who will appreciate them," as she spanked Cody into tearfully giving up his toys. That night after Cody was tucked in bed, Mrs. Smith told her husband, "Cody just doesn't know how *to share." This simple statement shed new light on the problem. The Smiths realized that they needed to teach* Cody what *sharing* meant.

The next time Cody's cousins came over, Mrs. Smith took him aside for a talk. "Cody, here's the new sharing rule. Anyone can play with anything in this house as long as another person is not holding it. If you or Mike or Mary is holding a toy, no one can take it away. Each of you may play with only one toy at a time." Mrs. Smith also told Cody that he could put away one favorite toy, which could belong to him and him alone.

The next few hours were tense for Mrs. Smith, but Cody seemed to be more relaxed. He began by holding only one toy and letting his cousins have their pick of the lot in the toy box. "I'm so proud of you for sharing," his watchful mother praised him as she oversaw the operation.

When she ventured off to fix lunch, the familiar "Mine" cry brought her back to the playroom. The new "burp-itself" doll was being pulled limb from limb by Mary and Cody. "This toy is causing trouble," Mrs. Smith stated matter-of-factly. "It must go to Time Out." The children stared in disbelief as they watched poor Betsy sitting in the Time Out chair looking as lonely as a misbehaved pooch. After two minutes, Mrs. Smith returned the toy to the children, who had long since forgotten about it and were busy playing with blocks.

As the weeks went by, the children played side by side with fewer Time Outs needed to restore peace, particularly since Cody was more open to letting "his" toys be "their" toys during the play period.

Not Wanting to Eat

Parents often find themselves pushing their on-the-go preschoolers to eat, since many children under six are too busy investigating their world to take much time out for food. If the temptation to force food on your child seems overwhelming, try giving her more attention for eating (even the smallest pea!) than for not eating.

Note: Preschoolers are notorious for their occasional bouts of not wanting to eat; don't mistake these for illness. However, get professional help if you feel your child is physically ill and can't eat.

Preventing the Problem

Don't skip meals yourself.

Skipping meals yourself gives your child the idea that not eating is okay for her, since it's okay for you.

Don't emphasize a big tummy or idolize a bone-thin physique.

Even a three-year-old can become irrationally weight conscious if you show her how to be obsessed with her body.

Learn the appropriate amount of food for your child's age and weight.

Growth rate, activity level, and physical size determine how many servings from the five food groups (milk, meat, vegetable, grain, and fruit) a child needs each day. Consult your child's health-care provider for answers to specific nutrition questions about your child. For more information about recommended guidelines for one- to five-year-olds, consult the National Dairy Council's website at www.nutritionexplorations.org.

Solving the Problem

What to Do

Encourage less food, more often.

Get your child's system in the habit of eating meals at particular times during the day. However, your child's stomach isn't as large as yours, so it can't hold enough food to last four or more hours between meals. Let your child eat as often as she likes, but only the right foods for good nutrition. For example, say, "Whenever you're hungry, let me know, and you can have celery with peanut butter or an apple with cheese." Make sure you can follow through with your suggestions, based on what foods are available and what time a bigger meal is coming.

Let your child choose foods.

Occasionally let your child choose her between-meal snack or lunch food (with your supervision). If she feels she has some control over what she's eating, she may be more excited about food. Offer her only two choices at a time, so she doesn't become overwhelmed with the decision-making process, and praise her choice with comments like, "I'm glad you chose that orange. It's really a delicious snack."

Provide variety and balance.

Children need to learn about proper diet, which involves a wide range of foods. Expose your child to the various tastes, textures, colors, and aromas of nutritious foods. Remember that preschoolers' tastes often change overnight, so expect your child to turn down a food today that was a favorite last week.

Let nature take its course.

A normal, healthy child will naturally select a balanced diet over a week's time, which pediatricians say will keep her adequately nourished. Keep a mental note of what your child has eaten from Monday through Sunday—not from sunup to sundown—before becoming alarmed that she's undernourished.

Catch your child with a mouthful.

Give your child encouragement when she downs a spoonful of nutritious food, to teach her that eating will bring her as much attention as not eating. Praise good eating habits by saying, "That's great the way you put that meat loaf in your mouth all by yourself," or, "I'm glad you like the rolls we have today."

Establish regular mealtimes.

Because your child is not on the same eating schedule as you, she may often want to play outside or finish block building when your mealtime arrives. She may need to be trained to switch to your schedule for sitting together. Do this *not* by forcing your child to eat a lot of food, but by setting a timer for the length of time she must remain at the table, eating or not. Say, "The timer will tell us when dinner is over. The rule is that you must stay at the table until the timer rings. Tell me when you're done eating, and I'll remove your plate." Let children under three stay at the table a shorter time (not more than five minutes) than four- or five-year-olds (not more than ten minutes). Identify the times when your child seems to get hungry, to learn what kind of hunger clock she's on (which you could switch to, if possible).

What Not to Do

Don't offer food rewards for eating.

Keep food in its proper perspective. Food is meant to provide nourishment, not to symbolize praise. Instead of offering your child ice cream for eating her vegetables, say, "Since you ate your green beans so nicely, you can go outside after dinner."

Don't bribe or beg.

When your child is not eating, don't bribe or beg her to clean her plate. This makes noneating a game to get your attention, which gives your child a feeling of power over you.

Don't get upset when your child won't eat.

Giving her attention for not eating makes not eating much more interesting to your child than eating.

Don't overreact.

Downplay the attention you give to your child's not wanting to eat so eating time does not become a battleground on which you wage power struggles.

"I Won't Eat!"

When John Rowland turned four years old, his appetite dropped to zero. His parents didn't know why and neither did his pediatrician, who checked him over physically at the insistence of John's fretful mother. One night, after Mrs. Rowland had begged him to eat just one pea, John threw a vehement tantrum, pushed his plate off the table, and shouted, "No, I won't eat!"

Mr. Rowland decided he had let his wife handle the situation too long. "Now, Johnny, listen to me. If you don't take a bite of macaroni, you'll have to leave the table," he threatened, firmly letting his son know the rule of the moment. He never guessed that Johnny would take him up on the offer and *get down from his chair. "Johnny Rowland, you will not get down from this table! You will stay and eat your dinner if you have to sit here all night!" Mr. Rowland yelled, changing the rules and thoroughly confusing his son.*

Later that night, after they had kissed and hugged their son and put him to bed, the Rowlands decided that something different had to be done— they did not want to spank and yell at their little boy for not eating. They wanted to turn mealtime back into what it used to be: a time for food and fun exchanges of stories, songs, and the events of the day.

The next night at dinner, they shifted their attention away from food and pretended to ignore John's lack of appetite. "Tell me about how you were the helper at preschool today," Johnny's mother began (with all the sincerity and calmness she could muster) as she passed the broccoli to her husband. John perked up as he told the story of how he was chosen to hold the flag. In between his excited explanations, he just happened to swallow a forkful of mashed potatoes.

"That was so nice of you to be such a good helper today," Mrs. Rowland complimented her son. "I'm glad you like the mashed potatoes, too," she added. The Rowlands continued their meal but refrained from pushing their son to try a few more potatoes.

The next morning John's parents discussed the evening's success and decided to continue what they were doing. They also remembered what John's doctor had said: "John may eat only small amounts, judging from his normal but slight body size, and he may eat those more than three times a day, as many people do."

Dinnertime became less of a daytime preoccupation for Mrs. Rowland. She began creating fun carrot-stick boats and cheese-and-raisin faces for John to eat throughout the day. John developed a whole new interest in eating more during the day, though he still only took a few mouthfuls at dinner. But the Rowlands appreciated those minutes John did spend eating, and they let their son dictate when he was and wasn't hungry.

Overeating

The appetite of many preschoolers can be as endless as that of the famous Cookie Monster on *Sesame Street*. Like the puppet hero, your child may not be aware of why he wants more food than he needs. But *you* need to understand his motivation in order to get his eating habits back on track. Because overeating is a symptom of a problem, not the problem itself, try to discover the reasons behind your child's seemingly bottomless pit. Possible explanations include habit, boredom, mimicry, or the desire for attention. Help him find ways to satisfy his needs and wants without overeating.

Note: Get professional help if your child is a consistent overeater. Avoid diets that are not medically supervised.

Preventing the Problem

Model a healthy attitude toward food.

Your relationship with food is contagious. When you complain about dieting or being too fat, for example, your child learns that food has power beyond making him healthy. Food becomes the enemy to defend against, lest he lose control and pig out on a forbidden chocolate cake. Since moderation is the key to health, moderate your talk as well as your behavior. Eating disorders in young children have become more prevalent, due in part to our dieting-obsessed culture.

Become well versed in what's appropriate for your child.

Growth rate, activity level, and physical size determine how many servings from the five food groups (milk, meat, vegetable, grain, fruit) a child needs each day. Consult your child's health-care provider for answers to specific nutrition questions about your child. For more information about recommended guidelines for one- to five-year-olds, consult the National Dairy Council's website at www.nutritionexplorations.org.

Serve healthy foods.

Keep both high-calorie and empty-calorie foods out of your overeater's reach so he won't be tempted to grab for them.

Check your child's diet.

Since your preschooler is too young to know what he should and shouldn't eat, it's up to you to establish healthy eating habits—the earlier the better. Foods high in fat and sugar should be replaced with those high in protein, vitamins, and minerals, to offer a balance of nutritious calories in a day.

Teach when, how, and where eating is allowed.

Restrict eating to the kitchen and dining room only. Slow down the eating pace and insist that food be eaten from a plate or bowl, instead of directly from the refrigerator. Taking more time between mouthfuls allows our brains to get the message that we're full *before* we've eaten more than we need. (This process takes about twenty minutes.)

Solving the Problem

What to Do

Provide pleasurable activities other than eating.

Get to know what your child likes to do besides eat, and suggest these activities after he's eaten enough to satisfy his hunger. Show him how delicious things other than food can be.

Keep food in perspective.

Don't offer food as a present or reward, to avoid teaching your child that eating means more than satisfying hunger.

Provide nutritious between-meal snacks.

A well-timed snack can prevent your child from getting overhungry and gorging at mealtime when it finally arrives.

Watch when your child overeats.

Try to discover why your child overeats by seeing if he turns to food when he's bored, mad, sad, watching others eat, or wanting attention from you. Help him resolve his feelings in noneating ways like talking or playing. Communicate with him about trouble spots in his life so he won't be tempted to make food a problem solver.

Control your own eating habits.

If parents snack on empty-calorie junk foods all day, their children will be inclined to do the same.

Praise wise food selections.

You can mold your child's food preferences by your tone of voice and by encouraging foods you want him to favor. Whenever your child picks up an orange instead of a piece of chocolate, say, "That's a great choice you made for a snack. I'm glad you're taking care of yourself so well by eating yummy treats like oranges."

Encourage exercise.

Overweight children often don't eat any more than normal-weight children; they just don't burn enough calories off through exercise. If you live in a cold climate, suggest physical activities to play inside in the winter, like dancing or jumping rope. In the summer, activities such as swimming, walking, baseball, and swinging are not only good for your child's physical development, they also relieve tension, give him fresh air, and build coordination and strength. Your participation will make exercise even more fun for your child.

Communicate with your child.

Make sure the encouragement you give your child to eat all his peas isn't the only encouragement you ever give him. Praise his artwork, the clothes he's chosen, the way he's cleaned up his toys, and so on to give him attention for things other than eating and overeating.

What Not to Do

Don't give in to his desire to overeat.

Just because your child wants more food doesn't mean he needs it, but don't make him feel guilty for wanting more by making fun of him and calling him "Little piggy," for example. To learn healthy portion sizes, consult the National Dairy Council's website at www.nutritionexplorations.org or ask your child's doctor for a nutrition plan. After you're sure your child has had enough, briefly explain why he shouldn't have more, because he's too young to tell himself the reason.

Don't give treats when your child is upset.

Your child may begin to associate food with emotional rather than physical nourishment if you consistently offer treats to ease his pain.

Don't consistently allow food while you're watching TV.

Avoid teaching your child to associate food with TV. Because television advertising bombards your child with food messages, it's also a good idea to limit his television viewing time.

Don't give junk foods as snacks.
What you allow for snacks and meals is what your child will expect. Food preferences are learned, not inborn.

Don't make fun of your child if he's overweight.
Making fun of your child only compounds the problem by adding to his guilt and shame.

"No More Cookies!"

Two-and-a-half-year-old Rosa Hanlon was getting a reputation at preschool and family functions for being a "walking bottomless pit." If food was in sight, Rosa ate it. She never seemed to be full.

"No, you can't have another cookie, Rosa!" Mrs. Hanlon would scream every time she caught her daughter with her hand in the cookie jar. "You've had enough cookies to last your lifetime!" But neither angry outbursts nor the threat of taking away her tricycle lessened Rosa's desire to finish every morsel in a box or on a plate.

Mrs. Hanlon decided to consult her pediatrician to learn how to change Rosa's eating habits. The doctor provided a nutrition plan and recipe suggestions specifically tailored for Rosa. The next day, Rosa asked for another helping of oatmeal after eating the suggested amount, but Mrs. Hanlon finally had an answer that wasn't angry or insulting: "I'm glad you liked the oatmeal, Rosa. We can have some more tomorrow morning. Let's go read that new book now."

Knowing that the amount she had given Rosa was nutritionally adequate made it easier for Mrs. Hanlon to stand firm when Rosa begged for more oatmeal. It was also easier for Mrs. Hanlon to plan each meal, because she knew what amounts were enough to nourish her daughter.

The Hanlons also reduced their steady supply of cookies, so Rosa started to try new foods that were tasty and more nutritious. Mrs. Hanlon praised Rosa every time she chose a healthy food. "That's great the way you picked an orange for a snack instead of cookies."

Rosa started to hear fewer comments about being a bottomless pit, and she received lots of hugs and compliments for eating fruit instead of fudge. Not only were her parents delighted to share exercise and fun with her, but Rosa seemed to have more fun with her friends and teachers, too.

Overusing *No*

No ranks as the most-likely-to-be-used word by toddlers because it's the most-likely-to-be-used word by parents. Toddlers are famous for getting into, on top of, and underneath things they shouldn't, and parents are famous for saying, "No! Don't touch!" "No! Don't open!" "No! Don't do that!" The best way to reduce the frequency of your toddler's use of *no* is by limiting her opportunities. Do this by avoiding yes-no questions and by not always taking her literally when she says no to every request.

Preventing the Problem

Get to know your child's personality.

If you're familiar with your child's needs and wants, you'll know when her *no* means no and when it really means yes or something else.

Think before saying "no."

Avoid telling your child "no" when you don't really care whether she does something or not.

Limit yes-no questions.

Avoid questions your child can answer with "No." For example, ask her *how much* juice she wants, not whether she wants some. If you want her to get in the car, don't say, "Do you want to get in the car?" Say, "We're getting in the car now," and do it!

Change your *no* to something else.

For example, say, "Stop," instead of, "No," when your child is doing something you don't want her to do.

Redirect your child's behavior.

Because you usually want your child to stop a behavior when you say "No" to her, teach another behavior to replace the one you want stopped. During a neutral time, take your child's hand and say, "Come here, please." Practice five times a day, slowly increasing the distance your child is away from you when you say, "Come here, please," until she can come to you from across the room or across the shopping center.

Solving the Problem

What to Do

Ignore your child's *no*.

If you're not sure what she means by *no*, assume she really means *yes*. For example, if she doesn't want the juice she just said "No" to, she won't take it. Eventually you'll know when she really means *no*.

Give more attention for *yes* than *no*.

Your child will learn how to say yes if nodding her head or saying "Yes" makes you smile and praise her. React positively by saying something like, "How nice of you to say 'Yes,'" or, "I'm really glad you said 'Yes' when your aunt asked you that question."

Teach your child how to say "Yes."

Children over three can learn to say "Yes" if they're shown how to do it. Tell your child that you want her to say "Yes." When she does, praise her with words like, "It's nice to hear you say 'Yes,'" or, "I really like the way you said 'Yes.'" Then say, "I'm going to ask you to do something for me and I want you to say 'Yes' before I can count to five." If she says it, tell her what a great *yes* that was. Practice this five times for five days and you'll be in for a more positive-sounding child.

Let your child say "No."

Even though she must still do what you want (or need) her to do, your child is entitled to say "No." When you want her to do something but she has said "No," explain the situation to her. For example, say, "I know you don't want to pick up your crayons, but when you've done what I asked you to do, then you may do what you want to do." This lets your child know that you've heard what she's said and are taking her feelings into consideration—but you're still the boss.

What Not to Do

Don't laugh or encourage the use of *no*.

Laughing or calling attention to your child's overuse of the word only encourages her to use it more to get your reaction.

Don't get angry.

Remember that the "no" stage is normal in your developing preschooler and will soon pass. Getting angry will be interpreted as giving your child attention for saying "No," and attention and power are just what she wants.

Negative Nathan

Twenty-month-old Nathan Shelby's favorite word to say was his parents' least favorite word to hear: no. Because little Nate used that word to answer every question asked of him, his parents started to wonder about his mental powers. "Can't you say anything besides no?" they'd ask their son, only to get his usual response.

So the Shelbys tried to reduce the number of times they used the word during the day, to see if that would have an effect on Nathan's vocabulary. Instead of saying, "No, not now," whenever Nate demanded a cookie, they said, "Yes, you may have a cookie when you've eaten your dinner." While they were still, in effect, saying no, Nate didn't react negatively in return. Instead, he took his parents up on their promise and got his cookie immediately after dinner.

As his parents traded in their no's for yes's, Nate started to increase his use of yes, a word that was immediately met with smiles, hugs, and compliments from his delighted parents. "Thanks for saying 'Yes' when I asked you if you wanted to take a bath," his mother would say. They were delighted that their son was decreasing his no's in direct proportion to how much praise he got for saying yes.

The Shelbys also tried to limit the number of yes-no questions they asked Nate. Instead of asking him if he wanted something to drink with his dinner, they said, "Do you want apple juice or milk?" Nate would happily make a choice between the two. Their efforts were painless ways to manage their son's negativism, and they soon found their household taking on a more positive tone.

Playing with Food

Take a one-, two-, or three-year-old, mix her with food she doesn't want to eat, and—presto!—you have an instant mess on your hands, her hands, and probably the floor and table, too. When your child starts playing with her food instead of putting it in her mouth, it usually means she's finished eating, whether she can say the words or not. Consistently take her food away as soon as it becomes a weapon or a toy, even if she's still hungry. This will teach her that food is meant to be eaten, not played with.

Preventing the Problem

Don't play with food yourself.
If you flip peas with your fork, even unconsciously, your child will assume that she can do it, too.

Plan food your child likes to eat.
To reduce the likelihood of a mess, cut her food into bite-size pieces that are easily handled and chewed.

Keep bowls of food out of reach.
Steer playful preschoolers away from the temptation to stir and pour just for fun.

Teach your child table manners at a noneating, neutral time.
Your child needs to know what you expect of her in restaurants and at home, because she didn't come built-in with table manners! It's best to teach her when you're not actually sitting down to dinner. For example, have frequent "tea parties" where you show her how to use her spoon, keep food on her tray, keep her hands out of her food, tell you when she's done, and so on. For a child under two, say, "Say, 'I'm done,' and then you can get down and play." For your three-, four-, or five-year-old, say, "When the timer rings, you can leave the table. Tell me when you're finished and I'll take your plate."

Talk to your child at the table.

If you make conversation with her, she won't find other ways to get your attention, like playing with food.

Solving the Problem

What to Do

Compliment proper eating habits.

Anytime your child is *not* playing with her food at the table, tell her you like how well she's eating. Say, for example, "That's great the way you're using your fork for those peas," or, "Thanks for twisting that spaghetti around your fork as I showed you."

Make playing with food unappetizing.

If your child breaks an eating rule you've previously discussed, tell her what the consequences are, to prove to her that playing with food is unacceptable. For example, say, "I'm sorry that you stuck your hands into your mashed potatoes. Now dinner is over."

Ask whether your child is done when she starts playing with her food.

Don't immediately assume that your child is being devilish. Ask her why she's dissecting her meat loaf, for example, to give her a chance to explain herself (if she's verbal).

What Not to Do

Don't lose your cool.

Though you may be disgusted and angry at your child for wasting her food, your anger may be the spice she wants with her meal. Your pre-schooler thrives on having the power to affect the world (for better and worse). Don't let playing with food become a way of getting attention. Ignore any nondestructive food play that you feel comfortable accepting at the table.

Don't give in.

If your child has to pay the price for playing with food, don't give in and remove the cost, even if she's screaming about how high it is. Teach your child you mean what you say every time you make a rule.

Dinnertime Disasters

Dinnertime at the Langners' looked more like art class than mealtime, since three-year-old Nick had begun smearing food around his plate and spitting out what didn't tickle his taste buds. His parents, who were disgusted with their son's wasteful games, tried to stop him by screaming, "Don't play with your food!"

Even after his mother threatened, "If you do that with your peas one more time, I'll take you down from the table," Nick tried to flip one more pea into his glass of milk. Spanking didn't bring any results either. Nick continued to eat only a few bites, after which he began feeding his frankfurters and beans to the nearby plants.

So the Langners decided to anticipate when Nick would be full. They noticed when his playful eyes and hands started to find new things to do with his French fries and green beans, and they quickly removed his plate. Nick's mother also spent a few minutes during the day teaching her son to say, "Through now," which he could use to signal when he was done eating.

Both of Nick's parents were relieved after experiencing three straight weeks without any food "art" at the table. But then Nick decided to try his hand at smearing creamed corn on the tablecloth. Fortunately, they had decided what the rule would be for slip-ups, and they calmly explained it to Nick. "Whenever you make a mess, you must clean it up." Instead of yelling at Nick, they calmly demonstrated the process.

Nick didn't get any attention for having to clean up his mess by himself, and it took only three wipe-up nights for him to start saying, "Through now." Those words worked like magic, he discovered, and he appreciated the hugs and kisses from his parents, who would say, "Thanks for saying, 'Through now,' Nick. I know you're done with your dinner and now you may go play with your trucks."

The whole family seemed relieved that more time was spent talking about how nice Nick was eating instead of how destructive he was with his food. Dinners with their son were shorter but sweeter than ever before.

Pretending to Use Weapons

Many moms and dads lament the fact that little boys, in particular, love to turn every object they touch into a weapon, from baseball bats to carrots, often imitating what they see on TV (with boys being more affected by violent TV than girls).[1] Young children do not process information the same way as adults, nor do they have the tools to evaluate what they see.

It has been reported that preschoolers who were given guns and other violent toys to play with acted more aggressively than preschoolers who only watched a television program with violent content.[2] But studies have shown that by the age of three, children will imitate someone on TV as readily as they will a real person.[3] The results of the studies on the effects of viewing television violence are consistent: Children learn how to be aggressive in new ways and draw conclusions about whether being aggressive will bring them rewards.

Those children who see television characters getting what they want by using weapons are more likely to imitate those acts themselves. If parents ignore or approve of their children's use of weapons or exhibit violent behavior themselves, they serve as role models for their children. On the other hand, parents who show their children how to solve problems nonviolently and who consistently praise their children for finding peaceful solutions to conflicts show their children how to be less aggressive.[4]

So when your preschooler makes pretend guns out of French fries, don't panic, but don't ignore his imaginative play either. Instead, teach the important lesson that even pretending to physically hurt people can hurt their feelings. Keep in mind that the behavior of the adults closest to a child encourages him to be kind or cruel. Watch what you do and say—and how "explosively" you act—in order to help curb your child's appetite for violent play.

Preventing the Problem

Make caring a household rule.

When your child behaves aggressively, make a rule that tells him what is or isn't allowed regarding pretending to use toys in violent ways. For example, say, "The rule is we treat people nicely to show them that we care. Pointing guns, even pretend ones, is against our rules because it hurts people's feelings and makes them afraid."

Think before speaking.

Use words and a tone of voice that you wouldn't mind your child repeating. For example, when he breaks a rule, instead of threatening (even in jest) to "knock his head off if he doesn't stop," calmly say, "I'm sorry you decided not to follow the rule about pretending to use a gun. The rule is, 'We treat each other nicely and don't ever hurt or pretend to hurt anyone.'"

Model kindness.

You are your child's first and most important role model. When you listen to, hug, apologize to, and respect your child, he will learn to behave in kind.

Learn to control your anger.

What causes children to "go off" is the same thing that causes adults to explode: anger over something beyond their control. Tell yourself you *hope* you get a raise, *hope* the traffic is light, *hope* your favorite dress still fits, and so on. But if none of these wishes comes true, don't have a meltdown. By keeping your cool, you set a powerful example for your child of maintaining self-control when things don't go your way.

Solving the Problem

What to Do

Teach empathy.

When your child pretends to attack another person with a toy gun or other object, consider this a teachable moment. Ask him to think about how it would feel to be shot by a pretend gun. Say, "Guns can hurt people. How would you feel if someone acted as if he were going to shoot you? I wouldn't want to scare or hurt anyone. I hope you wouldn't want to, either."

Encourage cooperative play.

Children who learn to enjoy building things, sharing with others, and engaging in supervised social activities will have less opportunity to resort to violent games for entertainment. Praise your preschooler when he's getting along with others while playing, so he knows you approve of his playing nicely. Say, "I like the way you're getting along and being kind to each other by sharing toys."

Restrict violent TV and video/computer games.

It's well documented that preschoolers like to imitate what they see. Many children have been victimized by kung fu kicks being tried out by playmates. In one Canadian study, children were found to be significantly more aggressive two years after TV was first introduced to their town.[5] Strong identification with a violent television character and believing that the television situation is realistic are both associated with greater aggressiveness.[6]

You need to know what your child is watching and what games he's playing. Reduce the amount of violent content your child is exposed to by making a rule about what he can watch or what games he can play as well as how long he can watch or play. Put yourself in charge of the television remote control and the computer power switch, to keep violence out of your home and out of your child's imagination.

When your child watches TV, watch with him.

Studies have shown that when an adult watches TV with a child and comments on the action, children remember more and are more likely to imitate what they've seen.[7] Because watching TV with an adult may actually intensify the positive (or negative) effect of the content on children, it's imperative that you select only nonviolent shows for your child's viewing and discuss the content with him. Your child should not watch with you if you're watching violent TV.

Teach your child to make amends.

When an overly exuberant tot tries to "shoot" a sibling or playmate with a ruler, for example, take away the "weapon" and say, "Guns hurt people. The rule is that we treat each other kindly and never even pretend to hurt another person. We don't hurt people; we love people. Please tell Sam you're sorry for pointing a gun at him." When your child follows your directions, say, "Thank you for being Sam's friend. I like the way you're showing him you care about him."

Teach your child to compromise.

Help your child learn to be fair when resolving disputes. When you see him threatening to hit his friend for taking his toy, for example, say, "Let's think about what else you could do when your friend takes your toy and you want it back. You could get the timer and set it like I do so your friend can play with the toy for a while and then you can play with it. That way both of you get to play with it and have fun."

What Not to Do

Don't hit!

No matter how tempting it is to spank a child to "smack some sense into him" or "teach him a lesson," resist the urge. Although you may be angry and scared when your child crosses the street without your permission, spanking him for doing so sends him a mixed message: It's okay for me to hit you, but not for you to hit me or anyone else. Practice what you preach. Spanking teaches him it's okay to hurt people to get them to do what you want. Even the occasional swat on the behind sends the hurtful message that if you're bigger and stronger, it's okay to hit to make a point.

Avoid overreacting.

When your child pretends to shoot his little brother with his pencil, for example, remain calm. Instead of simply forbidding the behavior, take advantage of a teachable moment by saying, "I'm sorry you broke the rule about treating people kindly. Tell me the rule and show me how you can treat your brother kindly now."

Don't threaten.

Threatening to hit your child with a wooden spoon when he's pretending to hit his sister with his stuffed animal only teaches him to fear your presence. To your child, a threat is an empty promise and an example of how adults don't keep their word. Instead of threatening a violent consequence such as, "I'll give you a spanking if I see you pretending to shoot your brother with that empty paper towel roll again," simply say, "I'm sorry you chose to break our rule about pretending to hurt someone. Now I want you to think about how scared you'd feel if somebody pointed a gun at you."

"Killer" Kyle

No matter what he got his hands on, three-year-old Kyle Liggett made it into a gun, knife, or sword. Then he shot, stabbed, or slashed away at any "bad guys" who were around. Kyle's mother, Diane, was beside herself. She was convinced that if she didn't bring play weapons into the house, her son wouldn't play so violently. Gary, Kyle's dad, only laughed about her fears. "Oh, Diane, boys will be boys. Why, I had toy guns when I was a kid, and you don't see me going around acting like I'm going to shoot people."

"But he makes a weapon out of everything," Diane lamented. "Today at

lunch, he bit his peanut butter and jelly sandwich into a gun and pretended he was shooting it at me. It was scary to see the mean look on his face as he was pointing the 'gun' at me."

"You should spank him when he does that," Gary responded. "That'd teach him not to point even a pretend gun at anybody."

"I'm not going to spank him," said Diane indignantly. "It doesn't make any sense to hurt *him to try to teach him not to hurt people. I was talking to Amy, Josh's mom, and she said that they got Josh to think about how others feel when a gun's pointed at them. She also made a rule that all kung fu cartoons and other violent stuff on TV were not welcome in their home. The TV went off whenever Josh chose that kind of garbage. She told me he got the message."*

"Well, let's try the same thing," Gary suggested. "By the way, I just thought about something else I should stop doing. You know how I'm always saying stuff like, 'If you do that once more, I'll rip your arm off!' I guess that sends Kyle the message that if a person is mad at someone, it's okay to hurt them."

Over the next few weeks, Kyle's parents squelched their violent messages. Instead of threatening him when he played pretend "shoot-'em-up," they said things like, "I'm sorry you're choosing to point guns at people. Guns can kill, and pointing guns at people scares them. Let's play school with that ruler instead of pretending to hurt somebody with it. Put the ruler on this paper and see what a straight line you can draw with your crayons."

"It's amazing," Diane told Gary. "I've been catching Kyle every time he uses a pretend gun and showing him something else to do with it. Now he's saying, 'Mommy doesn't like this TV,' whenever he sees somebody hurting someone on TV."

Gary laughed and said, "I overheard Kyle playing with Josh, and they started to pretend they were shooting each other when Kyle said, 'That's not nice to point guns at people. It hurts their feelings. Let's play with my trucks and stuff.'"

Kyle wasn't allowed to pretend to shoot someone at home, nor was he allowed to do so at preschool, church, or anywhere else. Although the Liggetts didn't believe that Kyle truly wanted to hurt someone, they knew that others might not be so sure of his motives. Sadly, children using violence against each other was not just pretend anymore. They wanted Kyle to understand that life is precious and it's wrong to hurt people, a message they hoped every child would be fortunate enough to hear from a loving parent.

Resisting Bedtime

Active, energetic preschoolers often do anything to avoid sleep. They turn bedtime or naptime into chase time, crying time, or finding-another-book-to-read time to postpone the dreaded bed. No matter what your child may think about the right time to sleep, stand firm with the time *you* have chosen. However, help your child gradually wind down instead of requiring him to turn off his motor instantly.

Note: Since your child's need for sleep changes as he gets older, you may need to let him stay up later or shorten his nap as he grows. Children (even ones in the same family) require different amounts of sleep. Your two-year-old may not need the same amount of sleep his older brother did when he was two.

Preventing the Problem

Establish a bedtime routine.

End the day or begin a nap with a special feeling between you and your child by reciting a poem or story as a regular part of the going-to-bed routine. Make the event special so it's something he can look forward to. Try reciting, "Night night, sleep tight, don't let the bedbugs bite," or have a talk about the day's events, even if it's a one-sided conversation.

Make exercise a daily habit.

Make sure your child gets plenty of exercise during the day, to help his body tell his mind that going to bed is a good idea.

Maintain a fairly regular nap schedule.

Don't let your child put off napping until late afternoon or evening, and then expect him to go to sleep at eight o'clock. Put him down for naps early enough in the day to make sure he's tired at bedtime.

Spend time together before bed.

Play with your child before bedtime arrives, to prevent him from fighting bedtime just to get your attention.

Keep bedtime consistent.

Determine how much sleep your child needs by noticing how he acts when he's taken a nap and when he hasn't, and when he's gone to bed at nine o'clock versus seven o'clock. Establish a consistent sleep schedule that meets his needs, and adjust it as he gets older.

Solving the Problem

What to Do

Use a timer to manage the bedtime routine.

An hour before bedtime (or naptime), set the timer for five minutes and announce that the timer will tell your child when it's time to start getting ready for bed. This avoids surprises and allows him to anticipate the upcoming events. When the timer rings, say, "The timer says it's time to start getting ready for bed. Let's take a bath and get into our pajamas." Then reset the timer for about fifteen minutes and say, "Let's see if we can beat the timer getting ready." This gives you the opportunity to praise your child's efforts at getting himself through the basic bedtime routine.

Make sure you allow enough time for him to get the job done. When the routine is finished, reset the timer for the remainder of the hour you set aside and announce, "You beat the timer. Now you get to stay up and play until the timer rings again and tells us that it's time to get into bed. Now, let's set the timer for brushing our teeth, getting a drink, and going potty (if he's old enough)." The timer routine helps you and your child make a game instead of a struggle out of bedtime.

Follow the same rituals regardless of time.

Even if bedtime has been delayed for some reason, go through the same rituals to help your child learn what's expected of him when it comes to going to bed. Don't point out how late he's stayed up. Quicken the pace by helping him get pajamas on and get a drink, and set the timer for shorter intervals. But don't omit any steps.

Maintain the same order of events.

Since preschoolers find comfort in consistency, have your child bathe, brush his teeth, and put on his pajamas in the same order every night. Ask him to name the next step in the routine, to make a game out of getting ready for bed and to help him feel as if he's calling the shots.

Offer rewards for going to bed.

Greet your child upon waking with the good news that going to bed nicely is worthwhile. Say, "Because you got in bed so nicely, I'll read you an extra story."

What Not to Do

Don't let your child control bedtime.

Stick with your chosen bedtime despite your child's resistance. Remember that you know why your child doesn't want to go to bed—and why he should. Say to yourself, "He's only crying because he doesn't want to end his playtime, but I know he'll play happier later if he sleeps now."

Don't threaten or spank.

Threatening or spanking your child to get him into bed can cause nightmares and fears, not to mention making you feel upset and guilty when the behavior persists. Punishing a child doesn't teach him appropriate behavior. Instead, focus on using a timer as a neutral authority to determine when bedtime arrives.

Don't be a historian.

Saying, for example, "Because you didn't go to bed on time last night, you don't get to watch TV this morning," doesn't teach your child how to get into bed on time. Focus on the future instead of the past.

Bedtime at Ben's

Evenings at the Shores' house meant one thing: a tearful battle of wills between three-year-old Ben and his father when the younger Shore's bedtime was announced. "I'm not tired! I don't want to go to bed! I want to stay up!" Ben would plead each night as his angry father dragged him to bed.

"I know you don't want to go to bed," his father would reply, "but you will do what I say, and I say it's bedtime!" Forcing his son to go to bed upset Mr. Shore as much as it did Ben. Even though Mr. Shore believed he should be boss, he knew there had to be a way to avoid the battles and Ben's crying himself to sleep.

The next night, Mr. Shore decided to control himself and let something else—the kitchen timer—control bedtime. An hour before Ben's bedtime, he set the timer for five minutes. "It's time to start getting ready for bed," Mr. Shore explained to his curious son. "When you get yourself ready for bed before the timer rings, we'll set the timer again and you can stay up and play until it rings."

Ben raced around and got ready for bed before the timer rang. As promised, Mr. Shore reset the timer, then read Ben his favorite animal tales and sang some new sleepytime songs until the timer rang again almost an hour later. "It's time for bed, right?" Ben announced, acting delighted to have this game all figured out.

"That's right! I'm so proud of you for remembering the new rule," his dad replied.

As the two journeyed up to bed, Mr. Shore once again told his son how proud he was of his getting himself ready for bed. Using the timer to control bedtime routines helped them enjoy a painless evening for the first time in months. After several weeks of following this routine, going to bed never became something to look forward to, but it was far from a struggle for Ben and his dad.

Resisting Car Seats

Car seats and seat belts are the number one enemy of millions of free-dom-loving preschoolers. These adventurous spirits don't under-stand why they must be strapped down, but they *can* understand the rule that the car doesn't move until the belts are on or they're strapped in their car seats. Ensure your child's safety every time she gets in a car by enforcing the belts-on rule. The seat-belt habit will become second nature to your child—a passenger today and a driver tomorrow—if you're not wishy-washy about this life-or-death rule.

Every state now requires that infants and children be buckled up when riding in a motor vehicle. Approved car seats and seat belts have weight and age specifications to make car travel as safe as possible for your child. Infants should be placed in rear-facing seats until they're at least one year old *and* weigh at least twenty pounds. As children outgrow their infant car seats, they move to forward-facing seats, convertible seats, and eventually booster seats, depending on their age and weight.

The leading cause of death in children is trauma from automobile accidents. Children who are not buckled up will continue to travel for-ward if the car stops suddenly. They will hit anything in their path—the dashboard, the windshield, or the back of the front seat—with an impact equivalent to a one-story drop for each ten miles per hour the car is trav-eling. Even though the dashboard and back of the front seat are padded, the impact of a crash at fifty-five miles per hour can do considerable damage to small bodies. This trauma can be prevented by making sure children are properly restrained. *Never* compromise the rule about being buckled up, or you may be compromising your child's life.

Note: The infant death rate can be reduced by almost three quarters and the injury rate for one- to four-year-olds can by lowered by fifty percent by using properly installed car seats. For more information on car seats, check the American Academy of Pediatrics website at www.aap.org or call 800-433-9016.

Preventing the Problem

Give your child room to breathe.

Make sure she has room to move her hands and legs and still be safely buckled up.

Make a rule that the car will not move unless everyone is buckled up.

If you enforce this rule from the beginning, your child will become accustomed to the idea of sitting in a car seat and eventually wearing a seat belt.

Make your child proud to be safe.

Tell your child why she's graduating to a bigger car seat or using only a seat belt, to make her proud of being strapped in. For example, say, "You're getting to be so grown-up. Here's your new safety seat for the car!"

Don't complain about having to wear a seat belt.

Casually telling your spouse or friend that you hate wearing a seat belt gives your child a reason to resist her belt, too.

Conduct a training program.

Let your child know how you expect her to act in a car. Take short drives around the neighborhood with one parent or friend driving and the other praising your child for sitting nicely in her car seat. Say, "You're sitting in your car seat so nicely today," or, "Nice sitting," while patting and stroking her.

Solving the Problem

What to Do

Buckle yourself up.

Make sure to wear your seat belt and point out how your child is wearing one, too, to make her feel she's not alone in her temporary confinement. If you don't wear a seat belt, your child will not understand why she has to.

Praise staying in the seat belt.

If you ignore your child while she's riding nicely, she may look for ways to get your attention, including trying to get out of her car seat or seat belt. Keep your child out of trouble in the car by talking to her and playing word games, as well as by praising how nicely she's sitting.

Be consistent.

Stop the car as quickly and safely as possible every time your child gets out of her car seat or seat belt, to teach her that the rule will be enforced. Say, "The car will move again only when you're back in your car seat [or seat belt], so you will be safe."

Divert your child's attention.

Try activities such as number games, word games, Peek-a-Boo, singing songs, and so on, so your child won't try to get out of her seat because she needs something to do.

What Not to Do

Don't attend to your child's defiant behavior, unless she unfastens her seat belt or gets out of her car seat.

Not giving attention to your child's crying or whining while she's belted in helps her see that there's no benefit in protesting the seat-belt rule. Say to yourself, "I know my child is safer in her car seat and will only fight it temporarily. Her safety is my responsibility and I am fulfilling it by enforcing the seat-belt rule."

Unbuckled Jacob

Stephen Brenner loved to take his four-year-old son, Jacob, on errands with him, until his son figured out how to get his father's undivided attention by unbuckling his seat belt and jumping around in the back seat. "Don't you ever undo that belt again, young man!" Mr. Brenner ordered when he saw that his son had gotten free.

Simply demanding that Jacob stay put didn't solve the problem, however, so Mr. Brenner decided that harsher, more physical punishment was necessary. Though he had never spanked his son before, he gave him a swift swat on his bottom whenever he found him roaming unbuckled in the back seat.

To accomplish the spanking, Mr. Brenner had to stop the car. Every time he did that, Jacob would scramble back to his seat and fasten his belt to avoid being walloped. So Mr. Brenner decided that instead of spanking Jacob, he would stop the car and refuse to continue until Jacob's belt was buckled. Mr. Brenner knew that Jacob wasn't patient enough to sit for very long, even if he didn't really want to go where they were going.

Mr. Brenner tried this new method the next time they were on their way to the park. When Jacob unbuckled himself, Mr. Brenner stopped the car. "We can go to the park when you're back in your seat and buckled up," Mr. Brenner explained. "It's not safe for you to be unbuckled." Mr. Brenner crossed his fingers, hoping that Jacob would get back in his seat, since Mr. Brenner knew Jacob was eager to get to the park. Jacob cooperated.

A few miles from home, Jacob unbuckled himself again, and Mr. Brenner stopped the car. He didn't spank his son; he simply repeated the rule. "The car will not move unless you're back in your car seat." Jacob returned to his seat and calmly buckled himself in. Mr. Brenner told him, "Thanks for getting back in your seat," and they drove home without incident.

That didn't end the problem, however. The next time Jacob released himself, Mr. Brenner was so angry he was tempted to yell and scream again, but he stuck to his new method. He also began to include Jacob in conversations and to praise his safe behavior. Soon after, Mr. Brenner was once again enjoying his outings with his son, assured that they were traveling safely.

Resisting Change

"**N**o! *Mommy* do it!" your son shrieks as your husband tries to give him a bath, a job he says is "*Mommy's.*" Change can be hard for people, but it's particularly difficult for the under-six set. It's even more trying for children born with a temperament that wants *everything* to be routine and predictable. Preschoolers haven't had much experience adjusting to change, so when you ask your little guy to get ready to leave when he's immersed in playing with a friend, he's likely to have a meltdown. Finding security in predictable sameness is common in little people, but sometimes the need for security borders on absolute inflexibility. Help reticent children learn how to go with the flow, to increase their chances of rolling with the punches as they grow.

Preventing the Problem

Provide a mistake-friendly environment.
By sending your child a no-big-deal message when he makes a mistake, you help him learn that no one's perfect. This lesson will serve him well as he gets experience bouncing back from a problem. Say, "I'm sorry you spilled your milk. Let's see how we can clean it up. Everyone has accidents."

Teach decision-making skills.
Your child wants to feel as if he's the master of his fate, so allow him to make simple decisions. Choosing between two cereals, two pairs of socks, and two games to play, for example, gives him a sense of control over his world.

Respect your child's individuality.
You may have made friends with change long ago, but your child might have a more difficult time because his temperament might be different. Understand that each child has a unique temperament, even within the same family. Avoid saying, "Don't be like that!" when your child's inflexible feathers are ruffled. Instead, say, "I know it's hard for you to change babysitters. But you can handle it. It'll be okay."

Remind children that they belong.
We all want to feel that we fit in with a particular group. So frequently tell your child that he's a valued member of your family, and encourage

his participation by asking him to help out around the house. Say, "Thanks for picking up your toys and putting them away. You're helping our home look nice and neat."

Solving the Problem

What to Do

Build resilience.

Resilient children look at change as a challenge to be overcome. On the other hand, inflexible children resist change as much as possible. Telling your child he *gets* to do something rather than *has* to do it will transform his feelings of fear and loss of control into feelings of excitement. Help him build this framework for change by saying, for example, "You get to have a new babysitter tonight. She's going to be lots of fun. Isn't it exciting getting to know someone new?"

Teach your child how to handle change.

Children who are shown how to deal with change are more prepared to meet the challenge. For example, say, "This new shirt is very nice. Not getting to wear your old blue one is no big deal. You'll feel so good wearing your new yellow one today."

Set goals for accepting change.

Children feel more in control of their destiny if they have ample time to think about and prepare themselves for change. You can help your child accept change more readily by having him set goals for handling change. For example, say, "We're going to the zoo with your class tomorrow. It'll be fun. Let's set a goal of having a good time at the zoo." Then periodically remind him of the goal and have him repeat it to you. Ask him, "What's your goal about going to the zoo?" When he says, "I'm going to the zoo to have fun," say, "That's right, you're going to the zoo to have a good time."

Teach problem solving.

When children are confronted with change and don't know what to do, giving them limited choices helps them see their options. For example, say, "I know you don't want to move into the big bed. Let's think about what we can do to make it easier. Maybe you could take your teddy bear into the big bed with you, and he'll keep you company while you're there."

What Not to Do

Don't meet resistance with anger.

Children who are upset by change need lots of support and empathy to reduce their anxiety. Getting angry with your child for being inflexible only increases his sense of helplessness.

Don't overreact to mistakes.

Getting upset when your child tracks dirt into the house tells him he isn't loveable if he makes mistakes, which (because he's a preschooler) he'll probably do many times a day. Treat mistakes as no big deal. Show him how to correct his behavior by treating mistakes as teachable—not terrorizing—moments. Say, "Please get the paper towels so we can clean this up. When we work together, we can have it cleaned up in no time."

The Cup and Bowl Caper

Julia Bardwell was only two-and-a-half-years old, but she had a mind of her own that belied her years. She knew what she wanted and how she wanted it, and her parents, Dena and Jim, knew better than to go against her wishes. If it wasn't a fight over using the blue cup instead of the yellow one at breakfast, it was a war over wearing something other than her green shorts and pink T-shirt. When confronted with change, Julia would first resist, then scream, and finally melt into an inconsolable, tearful tirade.

Dena and Jim wanted to help Julia become more resilient. Jim knew that setting goals at work helped him stay focused and not get distracted by his anxiety over getting everything done. He thought that Julia might be able to see beyond her fear of change if she had a goal to think about.

Dena and Jim decided that Julia's first goal would focus on her steadfast refusal to use different dishes at breakfast. When she could learn to be more flexible by using different dishes, they were hopeful she'd be able to be less rigid in dealing with other changes. So they began by talking to Julia about getting a new cup and bowl set for breakfast, one they let her pick out herself.

That night Dena said, "Julia, lets set a goal for tomorrow morning. I think it would be a good idea for your goal to be having fun using your new cup and bowl when you have breakfast." Julia looked at her mother and nodded, but Dena wasn't sure the idea of a goal had sunk in. A few minutes later, Dena said, "Julia, remember your goal for tomorrow morning? You're going to have fun using your new cup and bowl."

This time Julia answered, "Yeah, I 'member." The Bardwells repeated this reminder several more times that evening. They even made an occasional trip to the kitchen to look at the cup and bowl sitting all shiny and new on the counter.

At breakfast the next morning, Julia eagerly headed for the table saying, "Where's my new cup and bowl?" Dena and Jim knew they were onto something. They could help Julia accept change by helping her look forward to it. After a few days with the new cup and bowl, Dena and Jim said, "Julia, let's use the old blue cup and bowl at breakfast tomorrow."

"No!" Julia cried. "The new cup and bowl! I want the new cup and bowl!"

Dena and Jim didn't say anything about her digging in her heels like they had in the past. Instead, they decided to help her set a new goal. That evening Dena said, "Julia, let's set a new goal for breakfast tomorrow. I'd like your new goal to be using the old blue cup and bowl." Later that evening, Dena said, "Julia, what's the new goal for breakfast tomorrow?"

Julia thought for a minute and said, "The blue cup and bowl?"

"That's right," Dena said. "We're going to use the blue ones tomorrow. I'm glad you remembered the new goal."

Although Dena and Jim weren't sure this little exercise would pay off, they were delighted when Julia started treating it like a game and actually looked forward to the new goal for the day. They knew that Julia could ease into change as long as she was prepared for it. They now had a plan that made the whole family happy. Their perseverance had paid off.

Sibling Rivalry

Tattling on brothers and sisters and hating a new sibling from the first day he invades the family are just two examples of how sibling rivalry wreaks havoc on family relationships. Because preschoolers are constantly flapping their wings of independence and importance, they often fight with their siblings for space, time, and the number one position in their most important world: their family. Though sibling rivalry is part of human nature, its frequency can be decreased by showing each of your preschoolers that she's special. To keep sibling rivalry to a manageable minimum, teach your children that getting along gives them what they want: attention and privileges.

Preventing the Problem

Prepare your child before the new baby arrives.

Discuss with your first child (if she's over one year old) how she'll be included in the life of the new baby. Tell her what the new family routine will be and how she'll be expected to help out. This will help her feel that she's an important part of loving and caring for her younger sister or brother.

Play with your older child whether your baby is asleep or awake.

To decrease the sibling rivalry associated with a new baby, make sure you play with your older child when your new baby is awake as well as asleep. This will prevent your older child from concluding that you only give her attention when the baby's out of sight. Spending time with your older child no matter what the baby is doing makes your older child think, "I get Mom's attention when the baby's here as well as gone. That baby's not so bad after all!"

Make realistic getting-along goals.

Don't expect your child to smother the new baby with as much tenderness as you do. She may be older than the baby, but she still needs lots of individual attention.

Plan time alone with each of your children.

Even if you have half a dozen preschoolers to attend to, try to plan time alone with each of them (a bath, a walk, or a trip to the grocery store, for example). This will help focus your attention on each child's needs, and it will keep you informed about feelings and problems that may not surface amid the roar of the crowd at home.

Make individual brag boards (for parents of twins or children close in age).

Display each child's creativity in her own special place, to reassure each child that her efforts merit individual attention.

Solving the Problem

What to Do

Let a timer manage taking turns.

When your children are fighting for your undivided attention, let the timer determine each child's turn. This teaches your children about sharing, and it lets each child know she'll have a turn being your number one object of attention.

Offer alternatives to fighting.

Allowing fighting to flare up and burn out of control doesn't teach your children how to get along. Instead of allowing battles to be fought, give your children a choice: They can either get along or not get along. Say, "You may get along with each other and continue to play, or not get along and be separated in Time Out." Let them get in the habit of making choices, to give them a feeling of control over their lives and to help them learn to make decisions on their own.

Define *getting along*.

Be specific when praising your children for playing nicely together, to make sure they know what you mean by *getting along*. Say, "That's great the way you're sharing and playing together so nicely. I really like how you're getting along so well. It makes playing together fun."

What Not to Do

Don't respond to tattling.

Children tattle on each other as a way of enhancing their position with their parents. Stop this game of one-upmanship by saying, "I'm sorry you aren't getting along," and by pretending that the tattling didn't occur. Even if a dangerous activity has been reported, you can stop the activity and still ignore the tattling.

Don't set up one child to tattle on another.

Asking your older son to come tell you when his baby sister is doing something wrong is not a good way to teach your children how to get along without tattling.

Don't get upset when your children don't love each other all the time.

Children cannot live in the same home without *some* rivalry going on. It's human nature. Keep friction to a minimum by rewarding getting along and by not allowing the rivalry to escalate to fighting.

Don't hold grudges.

After the dispute has been settled, don't remind your children that they used to be enemies. Start over with a clean slate and help them do the same.

Starr Wars

The constant warfare between four-year-old Jason Starr and his two-year-old sister, Julie, made their parents wonder why they ever had children. The kids obviously didn't appreciate the sacrifices their parents made to buy them nice clothes, new toys, and good food.

Biting and teasing were Jason's favorite ways of letting his sister "have it" when he thought she was taking too much of his parents' time and attention. Physical punishment obviously wasn't working, since Jason seemed to want to get yelled at and walloped whenever he started hurting his sister.

The only time Mrs. Starr ever noticed her son being nice to his sister was when he helped her across an icy patch on the driveway. Mrs. Starr was so grateful for the bit of decency that she told her son, "That's great the way you helped your sister. I'm really proud of you." The Starrs decided to encourage more random acts of kindness by dishing out compliments when their children got along and by enforcing a new rule when their children began to fight.

They got the chance to put their new policy into practice later that day when a battle over blocks broke out after they got home from a shopping trip. Mrs. Starr had no idea who started the argument, but she told her children, "You have a choice now, kids. Since I don't know who took the toy from whom, you can get along like you did in the car today, or you can be separated in Time Out."

Both children ignored Mrs. Starr's statement and continued to play tug of war with the blocks. So she followed through with her promise. "You've both chosen to take a Time Out."

Julie and Jason screamed their way through most of Time Out, but after quieting down and being allowed to get up from their chairs, they had different looks on their faces for the rest of the day. They began to act like comrades rather than enemies, and Mrs. Starr was delighted that she had not lost her temper when her children had.

The Starrs continued to praise getting along. They put less emphasis on any fighting they noticed, and they consistently used Time Out to separate the children and reinforce the consequence of choosing to fight.

Taking Things

Since everything in the world belongs to a preschooler until someone tells him differently, it's never too early to teach him not to take things from others unless you approve it. Parents provide consciences for their children until they develop their own. So every time your child takes things that aren't his, enforce the consequences that will help him develop a sense of right and wrong.

Preventing the Problem

Make rules.

Encourage your child to let you know when he wants things by teaching him how to ask for them. Decide what may and may not be taken from public places or others' homes, and let your child know your expectations. A basic rule might be, "You must always ask me if you can have something before you pick it up."

Solving the Problem

What to Do

Explain how to get things without stealing.

Your child doesn't understand why he can't take things when he wants them. Make him aware of correct and incorrect behavior by saying, "You must ask me for a piece of gum before picking up the pack. If I say yes, you may pick it up and hold it until we pay for it."

Explain what *stealing* means.

Make sure your child understands the difference between borrowing and stealing (and the results of each), to make sure he knows what you mean when you say, "You must not steal." Stealing is taking something without permission; borrowing is asking for and getting permission before taking something.

Have your child pay for stealing.

To help him realize the cost of stealing, have your child work off the theft by doing odd jobs around the house or by giving up one of his prized possessions. Say, for example, "I'm sorry you took something that didn't belong to you. Because you did that, you must give up something that does belong to you." The possession he gives up could be used several months later as a reward for good behavior.

Make children return stolen objects.
Teach your child that he cannot keep something he's stolen. Enforce the rule that he must return it himself (with your help, if necessary).

Enforce Time Out.
When your child takes something that doesn't belong to him, let him know that he must be isolated from people and activities because he broke the rule. Say, "I'm sorry you took something that wasn't yours. Time out."

What Not to Do

Don't be a historian.
Don't remind your child about a stealing incident. Bringing up the past will only remind him of wrong behavior and won't teach him how to avoid the mistake in the future.

Don't label your child.
Don't call your child a "thief," because he will behave according to how he's labeled.

Don't ask your child whether he's stolen something.
Asking only encourages lying. He'll say to himself, "I know I'll get punished. Why not lie to avoid the pain?"

Don't hesitate to search your child.
If you suspect your child has stolen something, verify it by searching him. If you discover he did steal, make sure to enforce the consequences. For example, say, "I'm sorry you took something that didn't belong to you. Now you must pay for it."

The Short Shoplifter

Sandy and Doug Berkley had never broken the law and gone to jail, and they didn't want their four-year-old son, Scott, to get locked up either. But if he continued to steal gum, candy, toys, and other objects that caught his fancy while shopping with his parents, they wondered if he'd have a future outside of prison.

"Don't you know that stealing is wrong?" Mrs. Berkley would scream at her son when she'd catch him red-handed. She also tried slapping his hand and telling him he was a bad boy, but that didn't do any good, either. She became afraid to do errands with her son, dreading both the embarrassment of his behavior and how she would feel when she punished him.

Scott was totally oblivious to the reasons why stealing was forbidden. He didn't understand why it wasn't fun to take things that didn't belong to him. So the Berkleys decided to explain the situation in terms he could understand.

"Scott, you cannot take things that you do not pay for," Mr. Berkley began. "You must ask me for a pack of gum. If I say yes, you may pick up the pack and hold it until we pay for it. Let's practice." Scott was delighted to oblige because now when he asked for gum, as the rule stated, his mother and father complimented him for following the rules and paid for the gum.

But the Berkleys didn't always say yes to Scott's request. So when Scott tried to get by with taking a candy bar without first asking his mother to pay for it, Mrs. Berkley enforced her second rule by making him pay for the wrongdoing. "Because you took this candy bar," she told her son as they walked back into the store, "you will have to give up the toy candy bar that's in your grocery store at home."

Despite Scott's protests, Mrs. Berkley did take away his beloved toy. "To earn the toy back," she explained, "you have to follow the rules by asking first and by not taking what is not paid for."

After several weeks of praising Scott for following the rules, Mrs. Berkley gave him his toy candy bar back, and both parents began to feel more secure about their frisky little son's future.

Talking Back

When backtalk (sarcasm, sassy retorts, and unkind remarks) spews forth from your preschooler's previously angelic mouth, you become painfully aware of her ability to mimic words (good and bad) and control her world with them. Like other forms of language, backtalk can only be learned by exposure to it. So limit your child's opportunities to hear unpleasant words. Monitor television viewing, your own language, and that of friends and family.

Preventing the Problem

Talk to your child the way you want her to talk to you.

Teach your child how to use language you want to hear. Say "Thank you," "Please," "I'm sorry," and other polite phrases. Have your child practice using the words you've modeled. Remember that preschoolers are the world's greatest imitators.

Decide what constitutes backtalk.

In order to react fairly to your child's increasingly diversified verbal behavior, you need to determine whether your child is talking back or doing something else. For example, sarcasm, name-calling, shouting answers, and defiant refusals are backtalk. Simple refusals like "I don't *want* to" are whining. Questions like "Do I have to?" are expressions of opinion. Make sure your child understands what you mean by *backtalk*.

Monitor friends, media, and your own speech.

Limit your child's exposure to backtalk by keeping tabs on what words slip through your lips. Also monitor friends, peers, family members, and television characters. What goes in preschoolers' ears comes out preschoolers' mouths.

Solving the Problem

What to Do

Wear out the word.

Overusing a word reduces its power. Therefore, help your child grow tired of using an offensive word by having her repeat it (one minute for each year of age). Say, "I'm sorry you said that word. I'll set the timer. You must say the word until the timer rings. When it rings, you can stop saying the word." After the word is worn out, she'll be less likely to use it in the heat of the moment.

Ignore the backtalk.

Try to pay as little attention to inoffensive backtalk as you can. Pretending the event didn't occur takes away the backtalker's power over you. The game isn't much fun to play without the anticipated payoff of your reaction.

Compliment nice talk.

Let your child know what kind of talk you prefer by pointing out when she's using desirable language. Say, "I like it when you answer me kindly when I ask you a question, just as we practiced. That makes me feel good."

What Not to Do

Don't play a power game.

Since you know that backtalk is one way your child tries to get power over you, don't use backtalk yourself. She may find fun ways of entertaining herself by seeing how she can get you mad or get your attention by using backtalk, which you don't want to encourage.

Don't teach backtalk.

Shouting answers back at your child only shows her how to use backtalk. Although it's hard not to yell when you're being yelled at, teach your child how to be respectful by being respectful to her. Be polite to your child, as if she were a guest in your home.

Don't punish backtalk.

Backtalk is, at worst, annoying. No evidence supports the belief that we make children respectful by punishing them for disrespect. Only fear is taught through punishment—not respect.

Carlos' Backtalk

Whenever Mrs. Martinez would ask her four-year-old son, Carlos, to do anything like clean up his toys or put away the peanut butter, Carlos would shout, "No! I don't like you! I'm not going to!" Carlos became so experienced at backtalk and verbal abuse that whenever he was asked any kind of question, he would angrily shout back his answer, as if he had forgotten how to answer someone politely.

"No child of mine is going to talk like that!" Mr. Martinez would shout back at his son. Unfortunately, Mr. Martinez's backtalk would cause an even greater uproar in the family. Once the Martinezes realized their sarcasm and shouting were teaching their son this kind of behavior, they tried hard to react calmly to Carlos' backtalk and to praise his pleasant responses.

One day they asked Carlos to put his toys back in his toy box. When he calmly said, "Okay," they responded by saying, "That's really great the way you answered so pleasantly."

It wasn't hard for the Martinezes to control their anger. As Carlos' yelling and sassy talk became less frequent, they usually pretended they didn't hear it. But when Carlos kept saying "Idiot" over and over, trying hard to get some attention, the Martinezes decided to have Carlos wear out the word.

"Say the word idiot for four minutes," they instructed Carlos. Their son repeated the word for two minutes and then couldn't say it anymore. Much to the delight of his parents, it was the last time he said the word.

Temper Tantrums

Millions of normal, lovable preschoolers throw temper tantrums as their way of coping with frustration or anger, or of telling the world they're the boss. Tantrums can become less frequent and even be prevented by not giving the performer an audience and by not giving in to his demands. Though you may want to give in or crawl under the nearest checkout counter when your child throws a tantrum in public, be patient until he's finished and praise his gaining control after he's calm.

Note: Common, periodic crying is not a temper tantrum and needs to be treated differently. Get professional help if your child has more than two to three temper tantrums per day.

Preventing the Problem

Teach your child how to handle frustration and anger.

Show your child how adults like you can find other ways of coping besides yelling and screaming. When you burn the casserole, for instance, instead of throwing the burned pot into the garbage, say, "I'm upset now, honey, but I can handle it. I'm going to figure out how to solve this mess by seeing what else I can fix for dinner." Regardless of the situation, teach your child to look at the choices he has to solve his problems instead of getting violent about them.

Praise coping.

Catch your child being good. For example, praise his asking you to help him put together a complicated puzzle that might otherwise frustrate him. Say, "I'm so glad you asked for my help instead of getting mad at the puzzle." Helping your child handle his frustration and anger calmly helps him feel good about himself. You'll find him repeating a problem-solving technique when he knows he'll get praised for it. Tell him you understand his frustration by saying, "I know how you feel when things get tough, and I'm really proud of you for being able to solve the problem calmly."

Don't let playtime always mean alone time.

Pay attention to your child when he's playing appropriately with his toys, so he doesn't have to resort to inappropriate play to get your attention.

Don't wait for an invitation.

If you spot trouble brewing in your child's play or eating activities, don't let it simmer too long. When you see that the situation is difficult or frustrating for him, say, "I bet this puzzle piece goes here," or, "Let's do it this way." Show him how to work the toy or eat the food, and then let *him* complete the task so he feels good about his ability to let others help.

Solving the Problem

What to Do

Ignore your child's tantrum.

Do nothing for, with, or to your child during his performance. Teach him that a temper tantrum is not the way to get your attention or get his demands met. But how do you ignore a tornado tearing through your living room? Walk away from him during his tantrum, turn your back on him, put him in his room, or isolate yourself. If he's being destructive or dangerous to himself or others in public, put him in a confined place where he's safe. Don't even look his way during this isolation. Though it's tough to turn away, try to busy yourself in another room of the house or with another activity in public.

Try to stand firm.

Despite the power of your child's screaming and pounding, make sure you maintain self-control by holding tight to your rule. Tell yourself silently that it's important for your child to learn that he can't have everything he wants when he wants it. Your child is learning to be realistic, and you're learning to be consistent and to give him boundaries for acceptable and unacceptable behavior.

Remain as calm as you can.

Say to yourself, "This is not a big deal. If I can stay in control of myself, I can better teach my child to control himself. He's just trying to upset me so he can have what he wants." Keeping calm while ignoring his tantrum is the best model for him when he's upset.

Praise your child.

After the fire of a temper tantrum is reduced to smoldering ashes, immediately praise your child for regaining self-control, and get both of you involved in a favorite game or activity that isn't frustrating for him or you. Say, "I'm glad you're feeling better now. I love you, but I don't like screaming or yelling." Since this is your only reference to the tantrum, it will help him know that it was the tantrum you were ignoring, not him.

Explain rule changes.

If you and your child are at the store and he asks you to buy a toy that was off-limits before, you can change your mind—but change your message, too. Say, "Remember when we were here before and you threw a tantrum? When you behave nicely by staying close to me, I've decided that you can have the toy." This will help him understand that it wasn't the tantrum that changed your mind; you're buying the toy for another reason. If you like, tell him why you've changed your mind, particularly if it includes praise for his good behavior.

What Not to Do

Don't reason or explain during the tantrum.

Trying to reason your child out of his tantrum *during* the tantrum is wasted breath. He doesn't care. He's in the middle of a show and he's the star. Any discussion at this time only encourages the tantrum, because it gives him the audience he wants.

Don't throw a tantrum yourself.

Say to yourself, "Why do I need to act crazy? I know that when I said no, I said it for a reason." Losing your cool only encourages your child to keep the heat on, and it shows him that he doesn't need to learn self-control.

Don't belittle your child.

Just because your child has a temper tantrum doesn't mean he's a bad person. Don't say, "Bad boy! Aren't you ashamed of yourself?" Your child will lose respect for himself and feel that he didn't deserve what he wanted anyway.

Don't be a historian.

Don't remind your child of his tantrum later that day. This only gives more attention to the behavior and increases the chances of his having another tantrum, just to be the center of your conversation.

Don't make your child pay for the tantrum.

Having nothing to do with him after it's over will only cause him to have more tantrums to try to get your attention. Don't send him the message that he's unloved and unwanted just because his behavior was.

Tantrum Time

Donald and Mary MacLean were worried about their two-year-old daughter, Amy, who would get a bad attack of "temper tantrumitis" every time her request for a cookie before dinner was refused. When her parents said, "No," she would scream, "Yes!" pull on her father's pant leg, and jump up and down on the kitchen floor until both she and her distraught parents were so exhausted that they finally gave in.

In frustration, the MacLeans wondered what they were doing wrong. Was there something terribly wrong with saying no to Amy's demands? It finally occurred to them that Amy's tantrums were more frequent when they said no to her. They also realized that giving in to Amy's uncontrollable desire for a cookie before dinner only encouraged her bad behavior.

The next time Amy had a tantrum, they were ready with a new strategy. Instead of saying, "No," Mary said matter-of-factly, "Amy, I know you want a cookie, but you won't get one until you're quiet and have finished your dinner."

Amy didn't stop her tantrum, so her parents simply walked away, leaving her with no audience for her big scene. Although it was hard to stay away from their screaming child, the MacLeans waited until their daughter was quiet before entering the kitchen. Without any physical or verbal attention, Amy had eventually stopped wailing and was waiting to see if her parents would practice what they preached.

Her father appeared, wearing a smile, and said, "Amy, I know you want that cookie now, but when you've eaten your dinner and we're ready for dessert, then you may have the cookie. I'm glad you're not screaming and yelling now. It's nice to see you controlling yourself." Amy quietly went to dinner and, as promised, received her cookie when she was finished eating.

The MacLeans complimented themselves later that night on the self-control they had exhibited in not giving in to Amy's tantrum. Although they were tempted later on to give in, they continued to remove themselves from their daughter when she had a tantrum, and they praised her any time she reacted calmly when something was denied her. The frequency of Amy's tantrums diminished to the point that Amy would cry from time to time when she was disappointed, but she wouldn't have the explosive scenes she often had in the past.

Toileting Accidents

Toilet training is the first major battle of wills between parents and preschoolers. The war breaks out when parents ask their independence-loving offspring to give up something that is second nature to them and to begin doing something that is new and often undesirable. To most children, what is desirable about toilet training is pleasing their parents. So foster the least accident-prone toilet training possible by putting more attention on what your child *should* do (keep her pants dry, go to the bathroom in the potty) than on what she shouldn't do (go potty in her pants). Help your child feel proud of herself while you lessen the likelihood that she will have an accident just to get your attention and reaction.

Note: If your child is having continuous toileting accidents after the age of four, consult a medical professional. This chapter does not discuss bedwetting because many preschoolers are simply not developmentally able to stay dry all night. Many authorities believe that after age six, bedwetting may be considered a problem that requires professional help.

Preventing the Problem

Look for signs of readiness (usually around two years of age).

The generally accepted signs of readiness include a child's awareness of the fact that she's urinating or defecating (or is about to do so); more regular and predictable elimination patterns; the ability to pull her pants down and climb on the toilet (and do the opposite); the ability to understand toileting terminology and follow simple directions; an interest in toileting; and a general dislike of having a soiled diaper.

Don't train too early.

Early training simply teaches children to depend more on their parents than on their own ability to manage toileting. Children who are forced to learn before they're ready take longer to master toileting.

Model correct potty behavior.

Familiarize your child with the potty and how it's used by showing her how you go to the bathroom (and how she can when she's ready).

Make it as convenient as possible for your child to use the potty when she needs to go.

Keep the potty chair in the kitchen, for example, during toilet training. Take the potty with you in the early stages, to help your child feel comfortable about pottying outside the home.

Choose a toilet training procedure and stick with it.

Many resources (books, tapes, and videos) are available to help you toilet train your child. Find one that feels comfortable to you and consistently follow through with the recommended methods. Consistency and patience are the keys to success!

Solving the Problem

What to Do

Reward being dry as well as correct toileting.

Teach your child to keep herself dry by telling her how good staying dry is. This increases her awareness of what you want her to do (stay dry). About every fifteen minutes say to your child, "Check your pants. Are they dry?" This gives her the responsibility of checking her dryness, which makes her feel more in control of the process. If she's dry, tell her you're glad. Say, "How nice that you're staying dry."

Remind your child of the rule for going potty in wrong places.

Many preschoolers occasionally go to the bathroom in an inappropriate place (outside, for example). When your child has that experience, remind her that the rule is, "You're supposed to potty in the potty. Let's practice." Then proceed with practicing correct pottying procedures.

React calmly to accidents.

If your child is wet, say, "I'm sorry that you're wet. Now we need to practice staying dry." Then practice ten times going to the toilet from various parts of the house. (Pants down, sit on the toilet, pants up. Then repeat these steps in the next part of the house.) In practice it's not necessary for your child to urinate or have a bowel movement, but only to go through correct toileting motions.

Use Grandma's Rule in public.

When your child wants to go only in *her* potty when you're in a public place, try Grandma's Rule. Say, "We need to keep dry. One potty is the same as another. We can't use your potty because it's not here. When you've used this potty, we can go on a trip to the zoo." If you prefer, take your child's potty with you.

What Not to Do

Don't punish toileting accidents.

Punishment only gives your child attention for toileting in her pants (or another wrong place). It doesn't teach how to stay dry.

Don't ask the wrong question.

Saying "Check your pants" increases your child's awareness and puts her in charge. It's a good substitute for "Do you need to go potty?" which is generally answered with a "No." Help your child feel responsible for checking her dry-wet condition and doing something about it.

Kelly's "Accidents"

As soon as preschool let out for the summer, three-and-a-half-year-old Kelly Winter started to lose more than her knowledge of numbers and letters. Her occasional toileting accidents signaled that she was waiting too long before heading for the bathroom. Mrs. Winter watched her "dance" as she worked hard to avoid going to the bathroom.

Kelly discovered that she could relieve the physical pressure of having to go by releasing only a small amount of urine into her pants. When her mother would scold and spank her for wetting her pants, Kelly would point out how she wet "just a little." Mrs. Winter realized that Kelly wanted some attention for her accidents. Why else would she point out that she was wet "just a little"?

After analyzing the situation, Mr. and Mrs. Winter decided to reinstate the routine they had used to toilet train their daughter the previous year, and they began praising Kelly's dry pants instead of getting upset when she had wet ones. "Check your pants, Kelly. Are they dry?" Mrs. Winter said the next morning after breakfast. She was as delighted as Kelly when her daughter happily replied, "Yes!" with a big grin.

"Thanks for keeping yourself dry, honey," Mrs. Winter said, giving her daughter a hug at the same time. "Let's keep them dry all day!"

After a few days of periodically asking Kelly to check her pants (Kelly always found herself dry), Mrs. Winter thought her problem was behind her—until the very next day when Kelly was wet again. "Let's practice ten times going to the potty," she told her glum-looking daughter, who seemed very disappointed that her mother was not praising her as she did when her pants were dry.

Kelly soon learned that it was easier to go to the potty and get the praise for dry pants than it was to practice ten times. She continued to follow through with keeping her pants dry for several months.

Mr. and Mrs. Winter praised Kelly and occasionally reminded her during the next year. They kept in mind that Kelly had to firmly reestablish the right way of toileting, something her parents would rather help her do instead of become angry and frustrated when she soiled her pants.

Traveling Problems

For most adults, vacation traveling is a change of pace, scenery, and routine when cares of home are abandoned for the free and easy life. For many preschoolers, however, traveling is anything but vacation. Young ones thrive on the sense of security offered by familiar toys, beds, and foods, so try to prevent needing another vacation away from your child by making sure your preschooler knows that some of his favorite things (toys, blankets, clothes) will be near and that he'll be included in the fun. The comforts of home are often absent when you're traveling, so teach your child how to cope with change and how to enjoy new experiences—two tasks made easier if you have a happy, interested pupil who feels secure in his new surroundings.

Note: Remember that children who are not buckled in safely will create a dangerous distraction for the driver. If the car stops suddenly, they will continue to travel forward at the same rate of speed the car was going. They will hit anything in their path—the dashboard, the windshield, or the back of the front seat—with an impact equivalent to a one-story drop onto concrete for each ten miles per hour the car is traveling. Even though the dashboard and back of the front seat may be padded, hitting them from three to seven stories up (the impact you would have at speeds ranging from thirty to seventy miles per hour) could still be fatal. In addition, young children should *never* ride in the front seat of the car, even if restrained in car seats or seat belts. Always buckle them safely in the back seat in approved safety seats or booster seats. (See pages 110–113 for more on car seat safety.)

Preventing the Problem

Check the car seat or seat restraints before traveling.

The safety measures you take before leaving will determine how relaxed you are with your children when you finally depart. Don't wait until the last minute to find out you must delay your trip because you lack an essential item: the safety seat.

Practice the rule.

Before you and your child leave on a long-distance car trip, take a few dry runs so your child can graduate from basic training to the real thing. Praise proper sitting in the car seat or seat belts during practice time, to show your child that staying in his car seat produces rewards.

Make car rules.

Institute the rule that the car moves only when everyone is buckled in. Say, "I'm sorry your belt is not buckled. The car can't move until you're safely buckled in." Be prepared to wait until the passengers comply with your rule before you go.

Provide appropriate play materials.

Make sure you pack toys that are harmless to clothing and upholstery. Crayons are okay, but felt-tip pens are discouraged because they may permanently mark clothing and upholstery. If you're taking public transportation, provide activities that are quiet, usable in controlled spaces, and capable of holding your child's attention for long periods of time.

Familiarize your child with your travel plans.

Discuss your travel plans with your child so he'll know how long you'll be gone, what will happen to his room while you're away, and when you'll return. Show him maps and photos of your destination. Talk to him about the people, scenery, and events you'll experience. Share personal stories and souvenirs from previous visits to the destination. If your child is anxious about going to an unknown place, compare the destination to one he's familiar with.

Personally involve your child traveler.

Allow your child to participate in the preparation and execution of the trip. Enlist his help in packing his clothing, selecting carryon toys, carrying a tote bag, staying close in the terminal, and so on.

Establish rules of conduct for traveling.

Before you leave, explain to your child any special rules of the road. For example, you might establish a noise rule, an exploring rule, a pool rule, and a restaurant rule for stops along the way.

Solving the Problem

What to Do

Praise good behavior.

Frequently praise good behavior and provide rewards for staying in car seats. For example, say, "I like the way you're looking at all the trees and houses. It's really a pretty day. We can get out soon and play in the park because you've been sitting in your car seat so nicely."

Stop the car if your child gets out of his car seat or unbuckles his safety belt.

Make sure your child realizes that your car seat rule will be strictly enforced, and that the consequences will be the same every time the rule is violated.

Play car games.

Count objects, recognize colors, look for animals, and so on, to keep your child entertained. Make a list of fun things to do before you leave home. Switch games as needed, to maintain your child's (and your) interest.

Make frequent rest stops.

Your restless preschooler is usually happiest when he's mobile. Restraining him for hours in a car, plane, or train does not suit his adventurous spirit. Give him time to let off steam in a roadside park or rest stop, or you'll find him rebelling when you least desire it.

Monitor snacks on long trips.

Highly sugared or carbonated foods may not only increase a child's activity level, they may also increase the chance of nausea. Stick to protein snacks or lightly salted ones to keep him healthy and happy.

Use Grandma's Rule.

Let your child know that good behavior on trips brings rewards. For example, if your child has been whining about getting a drink, say, "When you've sat in your seat and talked with us without whining, then we'll stop and get something to drink."

What Not to Do

Don't let young children sit in the front seat.

No matter how much they fuss and beg to sit next to mommy or daddy in the front seat, young children should never be allowed to sit there, even on the shortest of trips. The safest place for preschoolers is buckled safely in a car seat or booster seat in the back, regardless of the type of air bag.

Don't make promises you may not fulfill.

Don't be too specific about what your child will see on your travels, because he might hold you to it. For example, if you say you'll see a bear in Yellowstone Park and you don't, you might hear whining such as, "But you *promised* I'd see a bear," when you leave the park.

Car Wars

Jerry and Andrea Sterling wanted to take their children on a vacation that was just like the vacations they had each enjoyed when they were young. But traveling with three-year-old Tracy and five-year-old Travis was more like punishment than a joy ride.

The back seat of the car became a fighting zone, and the children's screaming frequently led to threats and spanking. But punishment didn't seem to help. The Sterlings, who often felt just as angry after the punishment as they did before, felt nearly hopeless about finding a solution to their traveling problems.

Eventually they decided to develop new rules for traveling. They found some toys that their kids could play with without supervision; they explained the new policy for car trips; and they tested the rules on ordinary trips to the grocery store, park, and friends' homes. "Kids," they began, "we're going to the grocery store. When you've sat in your car seats and talked with us nicely all the way there, you can each pick out your favorite kind of juice."

The Sterlings praised their kids for initially following the rule. "Thanks for being so quiet. I really like the way you're not whining and hurting each other." But ultimately the plan failed and the kids didn't get a treat. However, it only took two more tests for the children to behave kindly toward each other and follow the car rules during the entire time in the car. They received praise for their efforts, and they were rewarded for their good behavior.

Two weeks later, the Sterling family began its two-hour trek to Grandma's, the longest trip in the car since the practice sessions had begun. The children knew what was expected of them and what rewards were available along the way and at their destination. This made going over the river and through the woods a lot more fun for everyone.

Wandering Away in Public

Curious preschoolers make mental lists of what to see and do at shopping centers, grocery stores, and so on, just like their parents. Preschoolers think their lists take priority, and chaos breaks out when their lists don't match their parents'. Your child's safety takes precedence over her curiosity in dangerous situations (getting in the way of cars, pedestrians, or grocery carts, for example), so enforce your rules about public behavior despite her protests. Make staying close in public a habit for your child until you can rely on her to know what is and isn't dangerous—a distinction she'll have learned from you.

Note: To foster your child's staying close in public, your emphasis must be on preventing any wandering. Once your child has left your side in public, the only thing to do is find her and prevent her from wandering away again.

Preventing the Problem

Establish rules for behaving in public.
At a neutral time (before or long after she misbehaves), let your child know what you expect of her in public. Say, "When we're in the store, you must stay within one arm's length from me."

Practice ahead of time.
Practice before leaving the house, so your child knows how to follow your rules. Say, "We're going to try staying within an arm's length of each other. Let's see how long you can stay close." After she does it, say, "Good staying close. Thanks for not moving away from me."

Teach your child to come to you.
During a neutral time, take your child's hand and say, "Come here, please." When she comes to you, give her a hug and say, "Thank you for coming." Practice five times a day, gradually increasing the distance your child is away from you before saying, "Come here, please," until she can come to you from across the room or across the store.

Praise staying close.

Make it worth your child's while to stay close by praising her every time she does. Say, "Good staying close," or, "You're being such a good shopper by staying close to me."

Involve your child in shopping.

Let your child hold a package or push the stroller, if she's able. This will make her feel like an important part of the shopping trip, and she'll be less tempted to roam.

Change your rule as your child changes.

As your child matures and becomes able to walk away briefly and come right back to your side in a public place like a shopping center, for example, you might change your rule and allow her to do that. Tell her why you're giving her more freedom. Knowing that she's earned more independence by good behavior in public will help her realize that following the rules is rewarded.

Be firm and consistent.

Don't change your public behavior rules without first telling your child. Being firm and consistent will give your child a sense of security. Your restrictions may occasionally produce some yelling and screaming, but the safety net you provide will help her feel protected in strange territory.

Solving the Problem

What to Do

Use reprimands and Time Out.

Reprimanding your child for not staying close in public will teach her what behavior you expect and what will happen if she doesn't follow your rule. When you see her not staying close, say, "Please stay close. You're supposed to stay with me. Staying close to me keeps you safe." If she repeatedly breaks your rule, restate the reprimand and put her in Time Out in a nearby chair while you stay with her.

What Not to Do

Don't let your child dictate your agenda.

Don't threaten to go home if your child doesn't stay close. Going home may be just what she wants, so she might wander away to get it.

Don't take your child shopping for longer than she can tolerate.

Some preschoolers can follow staying-close rules for longer periods of time than others. Get to know your child. One hour may be her limit, so consider that before leaving home.

Staying Put

Mr. and Mrs. Brody could not comfortably take their four-year-old son, Matthew, to a shopping center or grocery store anymore. He was always wandering out of sight as soon as his parents turned their backs. "Stay here! Never run away while we're shopping!" Mrs. Brody screamed at her son the last time he disappeared under a lingerie rack at the department store.

Her order proved ineffective. As they left the store and strolled down the mall, Matthew ran toward a shop window, pointed upward, and screamed, "Look at that train! Look at that train!" The shop window was almost out of hearing range, which caused Mrs. Brody to panic.

She realized that some rules needed to be established to prevent her son from disappearing while she did her holiday shopping. The next morning, she explained the new rule to her son before they went to the grocery store, because the grocery store was his favorite place to race from aisle to aisle. "Matthew, you must stay within arm's length of me while we're shopping," she began. "As long as you stay that close, you may look at things with your eyes, not with your hands."

During their trial run, Matthew was out of sight in minutes. "Remember the rule," Mrs. Brody told him when she finally caught up with him in Aisle 3 and pulled him close to her. "You're supposed to stay within an arm's length of me. Staying close to me keeps you safe."

Matthew acted like he didn't hear what she was saying, taking off toward his beloved granola bars. Mrs. Brody, boiling inside but cool on the surface, told herself that the rules were new. Like all new rules, they'd need practice before they'd be followed perfectly. "You're supposed to stay with me because staying close keeps you safe," she repeated. Then she walked him to the quiet corner by the produce and turned her back on him while staying near.

Matthew glared at his mother in protest, yelling, "No! I want to play. I don't like you!" Embarrassed but unflinching, Mrs. Brody ignored his outburst. She decided that if a reprimand didn't solve the problem, she'd put her son in Time Out to help him learn the rule.

At the end of three minutes (which seemed like three hours to Mrs. Brody), she greeted Matthew with a smile and reviewed the rule as they finished shopping. Whenever Matthew stayed within arm's length, Mrs. Brody praised him. "Thanks for staying close, honey. I'm really glad we're shopping together." They began talking about cereals and planning which ones to buy for breakfast that week.

Mrs. Brody consistently reminded him of the rule over the next few weeks, but she rarely had to use Time Out because they were having so much fun enjoying the new closeness between them.

Wanting Their Own Way

Because patience is not an innate virtue, young children must be taught the art of waiting for what they want. Because *you* are more experienced in knowing what's best for your preschooler, you're more qualified to control when he can do what he wants to do and what conditions must be met before he does it. Explain these conditions clearly. For example, say, "I know you want to eat the cake batter, but you don't need it now. When you wait until it's baked, it will turn into more cake for you to eat."

Also, show him how having patience pays off in your life, too. Say, for instance, "I know it's unpleasant for me to wait to buy the new dining-room furniture I want, but I know that if I work hard at saving money, I'll be able to buy it soon." Your child is just discovering that the world will not always revolve around his desires. It's not too soon for him to start learning how to cope with this often frustrating fact of life.

Preventing the Problem

Provide a menu of activities from which your child may choose.

Set up conditions that must be satisfied before your child gets his own way, and provide him with suggestions for activities he can do while he's waiting for what he wants. For example, say, "When you've played with the pegs for five minutes, then we'll go to Grandma's."

Solving the Problem

What to Do

Encourage patience.

Reward even the slightest sign of patience by telling your child how glad you are he waited. Define *patience* if you think he might not be familiar with the word. For example, say, "You're being so patient by waiting calmly for your drink until I clean the sink. That shows me how grown-up you are." This teaches your child that he *does* have the ability to put off his wants, even though he doesn't know it yet. It also helps him feel good about himself, because you feel good about his behavior.

Remain as calm as you can.

If your child protests waiting or not having things his own way, remind yourself that he's learning a valuable lesson for living: the art of patience. By seeing you be patient, he'll soon learn that demanding doesn't get his wants satisfied as quickly as getting the job done.

Use Grandma's Rule.

If your child is screaming, "Go! Go! Go to the park!" simply state the conditions he must meet in order to satisfy his wants. Be positive. For example, say, "When you've put the books back on the bookshelf, we'll go to the park."

Avoid a flat "No."

Whenever it's possible and safe, tell your child how he can have his own way. Avoid making him feel that his desires will never be satisfied. For example, say, "When you've washed your hands, then you may have an apple." Sometimes, of course, you need to say no to your child (when he wants to play with your lawnmower, for instance). At those times, try to offer alternative playthings to satisfy his wishes and to foster a sense of compromise and flexibility.

What Not to Do

Don't demand that your child do something "now."

Demanding that your child immediately do what you want contradicts the lesson you're trying to teach. If you don't want him to demand instant results, don't do it yourself.

Don't reward impatience.

Don't give in to your child's desires every time he wants his own way. Although it may be tempting to do so in order to avoid a battle or a tantrum, constantly giving in only reinforces his impatient behavior and fails to teach him patience.

Make sure your child knows it's not his demanding that got his wants fulfilled.

Though your child may moan and groan throughout the waiting time, make sure he knows that you're getting in the car because you're ready and your jobs are done, not because he wailed his way out the door. Say, "I've finished washing the dishes. Now we can go."

"I Want It Now!"

"Drink now!" two-year-old Emily Randolph wailed every time she was thirsty. When she saw her mother giving a bottle to her new baby brother, Justin, she wanted one, too—immediately.

"No, I'm busy. You'll just have to wait!" her mother responded, growing impatient with her daughter for not understanding that babies don't know how to wait for what they want.

Emily made so many demands to be held or given toys or drinks that Mrs. Randolph began to dread the moment when Emily would enter the room while her mother was busy with anything, especially taking care of Justin. When Emily began taking food, drinks, toys, and blankets away from Justin, saying that they were "mine," Mrs. Randolph realized that she needed to fix the problem. She declared a new rule, called Grandma's Rule, and explained it to Emily: "When you do what I ask you to do, then you may do what you want to do. This is the new rule."

That afternoon, Emily insisted on having a drink only ten minutes after the last one. Mrs. Randolph stated firmly, "When you put your shoes on, then you may have some apple juice." Emily was used to hearing, "No," and then throwing a tantrum until her mother gave in, so she ignored the new rule and continued to plead, "I'm thirsty!"

Not only did her tantrum not bring a drink, it caused Mrs. Randolph to ignore Emily completely. The frustrated girl finally put on her shoes to see if that would bring her the attention (and drink) she wanted, since screaming had not. She was surprised and delighted when it did.

Emily quickly learned that her mother meant what she said, because she never strayed from enforcing Grandma's Rule. When Emily fulfilled her part of the bargain, Mrs. Randolph praised her accomplishments with comments like, "I'm so glad you cleared the dishes from the table. You can go outside now."

Mrs. Randolph's admiration was sincere. Emily appreciated it and became more responsive to her mother's rules, which Mrs. Randolph tried to limit whenever possible. As the family learned to work together to satisfy everyone's needs, they grew to enjoy living with—not in spite of—each other.

Whining

Just as adults occasionally find themselves in a bad mood for no apparent reason, preschoolers are sometimes whiny and cranky even though their physical needs have been met. This behavior is usually the result of your child wanting attention or wanting her own way. Though it may be hard to do, ignoring the whining does help wind it down. Your child will soon learn an important rule: Asking nicely speaks louder than being cranky and noncommunicative.

Preventing the Problem

Catch 'em being pleasant.
When your child is not whining, tell her how much you like being with her. Your attention teaches her the rewards of a positive attitude.

Keep her needs met.
Make sure your child eats, bathes, dresses, sleeps, and gets plenty of hugs on a regular basis, to prevent her from becoming cranky because she's wet, hungry, overtired, or too upset to tell you her feelings without whining.

Solving the Problem

What to Do

Define *whining*.
Make sure your child knows exactly what you mean by *whining*. Then explain how you'd like her to ask for something or tell you what she wants without whining. For example, say, "When you ask nicely, I'll give you some apple juice. Here's how I'd like you to ask: 'Mommy [or Daddy], may I please have some apple juice?'" If your child isn't talking yet, show her how to indicate what she wants by using actions or gestures. Let her practice requesting things pleasantly at least five times. Make sure you fulfill her request, to prove your point that asking nicely gets results.

Create a "whining place," if necessary.
If your child's whining continues even after you've taught her how to express her wants nicely, let her know that she has the right to have

feelings and frustrations that only whining can relieve. Tell her that she can whine as much as she wants, but that she must do it in the "whining place," an area designated for whining. Let her know that you'd rather not be around a whiner who can't tell you what she wants, and when she's done whining she can come out. Say, "I'm sorry you're so upset. You can go to the whining place and come back when you're feeling better."

Ignore your child's whining.

Because your child's whining is so nerve-racking, you can easily pay more attention to her when she's whining than when she's quiet, even though that attention is not affection. After you've put her in the whining chair and given her the go-ahead to get the frustration out of her system, put on headphones or do something else to help yourself ignore the whining until it's over.

Point out nonwhining times.

To show your child the vivid contrast between how you react when she does and doesn't whine, immediately praise her quieting down by saying, "You're being so pleasant! Let's go get a toy!" or, "I haven't heard you whine for the longest time!" or, "Thanks for not whining!"

What Not to Do

Don't give in to the whining.

If you give your whining child attention by getting upset or giving her what she's whining for, you're teaching her that whining is the way to get what she wants.

Don't whine yourself.

Adult complaining may sound like whining to a child. If you're doing it, your preschooler may think it's okay for her. If you're in a bad mood, don't get angry with your child because you're angry with the world. Simply tell her that you're feeling out of sorts; don't whine about it.

Don't get angry with your child.

Don't get angry with your child because she's having an "off" day. She'll not only mistake your outbursts for attention, she'll feel a sense of power over you because she's made you mad. She may continue to whine just to show you she's the boss.

Don't punish your child for whining.

The old retort "I'll give you something to really whine about" only creates conflict between you and your child. It tells her that it's never okay to whine, which makes her feel guilty for having disgruntled feelings. Allow whining with restrictions, because whining may be the only way your child can vent frustrations at the time.

Remember, this won't last forever.
Your child may be having a bad day or going through a period when nothing seems to please her, so she may spend more time whining until she gets back in sync with her world. Tell yourself, "This too shall pass," while you try to lift her spirits by praising her good behavior.

The Whining Chair

From the moment three-year-old Aisha Gonzalez woke up in the morning until she closed her eyes at night, she was a constant whirlwind of whining. "Mommy, I wanna eat! Mommy, what's on TV? Mommy, where are we going? Mommy, pick me up!"

Mrs. Gonzalez tried to ignore her daughter's noisemaking, but she frequently gave in to Aisha's demands in order to get her to be quiet. But the whining and whimpering started to grate on Mrs. Gonzalez's nerves until one day she screamed, "Aisha, stop that stupid whining. You sound horrible!"

Yelling at Aisha only increased her whining, so Mrs. Gonzalez decided she'd have to use a different method. She decided to try a variation of Time Out, a technique she'd used whenever her daughter misbehaved.

"This is the whining chair," she told Aisha the next morning after she began her regular whining routine. "I'm sorry you're whining now. You must sit here until you're finished whining. When you're done, you can get up and we'll play with your dolls." She placed her daughter in the chair she had selected for this purpose. Then she walked away, making sure she wasn't around to give her daughter any attention. When she heard the whining stop, she returned to her daughter and praised her. "Oh, I love the way you're not whining. Let's go play."

When Mrs. Gonzalez realized her daughter was going to the whining chair nearly ten times a day, she decided to take the next step and teach Aisha how to stop herself from being put in the whining chair. "When you ask me nicely, I'll give you a drink," she explained. Then she taught Aisha how to ask nicely: "Please, Mom, may I have a drink?"

Her daughter practiced these instructions whenever she wanted something she had previously whined for. Though Aisha's whining never completely disappeared (she still whined on her "off" days), Mrs. Gonzalez became much happier with her relationship with her daughter.

Appendix I: Childproofing Checklist

Alarming statistics show that accidents are the number one cause of death in young children. Most accidents occur as a result of children's normal, healthy curiosity. Chances of getting hurt increase as children creep, crawl, walk, climb, and explore. The following checklist identifies steps parents should take to prevent home accidents:

- Always keep guns and knives locked safely away from children. Each gun should have its own trigger lock, and ammunition should be locked in a separate location out of reach of little hands.
- Install childproof latches on all cabinets and drawers that contain dangerous objects.
- Crawl through the house on your hands and knees to spot enticing hazards to be remedied.
- Plug empty electrical outlets with plastic plugs designed for this purpose.
- Remove unused extension cords.
- Move large pieces of furniture in front of electrical outlets that have cords plugged in them, or install protective outlet coverings that prevent a child from unplugging the cord.
- If small tables or other furnishings are not sturdy or have sharp corners, put them away until your child is older, or install protective coverings around sharp edges.
- Large pieces of furniture that a child can climb and tip over should be safely secured to a nearby wall.
- Place dangerous household substances, such as detergents, cleaning fluids, razor blades, matches, and medicines, well out of reach in a locked cabinet.
- Install a proper screen on a fireplace.
- Always use a correct car seat in your automobile.
- Regularly check toys for sharp edges or small broken pieces.
- Check the floor for small objects that your child could swallow or choke on.
- Put a gate on a stairway to prevent unsupervised play on the stairs.
- Never leave your baby unattended on a changing table, in the bathtub, on a couch, on your bed, in an infant seat or highchair, on the floor, or in a car.
- Have syrup of ipecac on hand to induce vomiting in case your child swallows a noncorrosive poison.

- Place small, fragile tabletop items out of your child's reach.
- Keep the door to the bathroom closed at all times. Use a childproof doorknob cover if your child knows how to turn the doorknob.
- Install safety latches on toilet lids.
- Keep plastic bags and small objects (pins, buttons, nuts, hard candy, money) out of reach at all times.
- Make sure toys, furniture, and walls are finished in lead-free paint. Check labels to make sure toys are nontoxic.
- Teach the word *hot* as early as you can. Keep your child away from the hot oven, iron, vent, fireplace, wood stove, barbecue grill, cigarettes, cigarette lighter, and hot teacups and coffee cups.
- Always turn pot handles inward when cooking, and remove gas knobs on the stove when not in use.
- Install safety latches for stand-alone freezers and oven doors, if they don't have locks.
- Always raise crib sides in the up position when your baby (even a tiny infant) is in the crib.
- Do not hang a tablecloth off a table when your small child is close by.
- Never tie toys to a crib or playpen. Your baby could strangle on the string. Also, never attach a pacifier to a string that could get wrapped around your baby's neck.

Appendix II: Is My Child Hyperactive?

If you suspect your child is hyperactive, the following guidelines will help you know what to expect when his behavior is evaluated. Only a detailed picture of your child and how he navigates his world can lead to an appropriate diagnosis and effective treatment plan. When conducting a thorough evaluation, a trained mental health professional (psychologist, social worker, psychiatrist) will gather information in the following areas:

A. Family history, including:
1. Your child's developmental, school, and treatment history
2. Your family's psychiatric history
3. All previous diagnostic screenings done on your child
4. Behavior checklists completed by parents, teachers, and so on
5. Your child's social functioning at home, in the neighborhood, and at school
6. How your family understands and reacts to your child's behavior
7. Your child's sleep patterns
8. Your child's diet and allergies
9. An analysis of the factors related to your child's behavior, including:
   a. How your child interacts with his mother, father, siblings, peers, teachers, coaches, and so on
   b. How your child reacts at home, in school, at social gatherings, in the neighborhood, and so on
   c. How your child reacts to reading, writing, homework, video games, getting dressed, and so on
   d. How your child behaves early in the morning, after school, during meals, when he's bored, at bedtime, and so on

B. An interview with your child to gather the following information:
1. His understanding of and thoughts about his problems
2. His general emotional functioning

C. An analysis of your child's behavior in school, including:
   1. Teacher-completed behavior checklists
   2. Teachers' understanding of and reaction to your child's behavior
   3. Classroom observation of your child across several tasks and settings

D. Formal testing to evaluate the following:
   1. General cognitive functioning
   2. Achievement skills
   3. Attention to task
   4. Language processing
   5. Sensory-motor skills

References

Introduction

1. Lawrence Kohlberg, "Moral Stages and Moralization: The Cognitive-Developmental Approach," in T. Lickona (ed.), *Moral Development and Behavior*, Holt, Rinehart, and Winston (1976).

2. Harriet H. Barrish, Ph.D., and I. J. Barrish, Ph.D., *Managing Parental Anger*, Overland Press (1985).

3. Richard Rhodes, *Why They Kill: The Discoveries of a Maverick Criminologist*, Alfred A. Knopf (1999).

4. Beth Azar, "Defining the Trait That Makes Us Human," *APA Monitor*, Vol. 28, No. 11 (November 1997).

5. Barbara Unell and Jerry Wyckoff, *20 Teachable Virtues*, Perigee Books (1995).

Pretending to Use Weapons

1. M. M. Lefkowitz, L. D. Eron, L. D. Walder, and L. R. Huesmann, *Growing Up to Be Violent*, Pergamon Press (1977).

2. R. Potts, A. C. Houston, and J. C. Wright, "The Effects of Television for and Violent Content on Boys' Attention and Social Behavior," *Journal of Experimental Child Psychology*, 41 (1986): 1–17.

3. R. B. McCall, R. D. Parke, and R. D. Kavanaugh, "Imitation of Live and Televised Models by Children One to Three Years of Age," *Monographs of the Society for Research in Child Development*, 42, Serial No. 173 (1977).

4. D. Singer and J. Singer, "Family Experiences and Television Viewing As Predictors of Children's Imagination, Restlessness, and Aggression," *Journal of Social Issues*, 42 (1986): 107–24.

5. L. A. Joy, M. M. Kimball, and M. L. Zabrack, "Television and Children's Aggressive Behaviour," in T. T. Williams (ed.), *The Impact of Television: A Natural Experiment in Three Communities*, Academic Press (1986).

6. L. R. Huesmann, "Psychological Processes Promoting the Relation between Exposure to Media Violence and Aggressive Behavior by the Viewer," *Journal of Social Issues,* 42 (1986): 125–39.

7. J. E. Grusec, "Effects of Co-Observer Evaluations of Imitation: A Developmental Toleration of Real-Life Aggression?" *Developmental Psychology,* 10 (1973): 418–21.

Index

lying and, 68
teaching, violence and, 102
Exercise
bedtime resistance and, 106
hyperactivity and, 54
overeating and, 93
Exploring, 46–48

F

Fear of strangers, 57, 58
Following directions, 79–82
Food
eating too much, 91–94
on long trips, 138
not wanting to eat, 87–90
playing with, 98–100
rewarding with, 23
television and, 23
Freedom, demanding, 32–34
Friendliness, 58

G

Games and activities
car, 138
for clinging to parents, 25–26
creative, 22
for dawdling, 29–30
for experiencing jealousy, 64
hyperactivity and, 52–53
physical, 22, 23
while waiting, 144
See also Play; Toys
Getting along
defining for child, 119
praising, 16, 102, 120, 121
Getting into things, 46–48
Getting out of bed at night, 49–51
Girl-boy differences, 8–9
Grandma's Rule
for cleaning up, 73
for cleanup (hygienic) routine, 44
for dawdling, 30
defined, 13
for following directions, 80
for interrupting, 61
for toilet training, 133–34
for travel behavior, 138
for wanting their own way, 145, 146
Grounding, 54

Guns, keeping locked up, 47
See also Weapons

H

Hitting, 15, 16
See also Spanking
Hyperactivity, 52–56, 152–53

I

Independence
demanding, 35–38
helping with siblings and, 64
taking directions from others and, 79
Interrupting, 60–62

J

Jealousy, 63–66

K

Kindness, modeling, 102
Knives, keeping locked up, 47
Kohlberg, Lawrence, 5

L

Labels
liar, 70
shy, 20, 21
thief, 123
Language
backtalk, 125–27
name-calling, 76–78
Limits
establishing, 32
physical, 46
rewards/consequences for, 33
Lying, 67–71

M

Make amends, teaching child to, 103
Make-believe play, 69
Medication, 54
Messiness, 72–75
"Mine," 83
Mistakes
criticism and punishment for, 37
resistance to change and, 114

N

Name-calling, 76–78

Busy Books

Each busy book contains 365 activities (one for each day of the year) for your children using items found around the home. The books offer parents and child-care providers fun reading, math, and science activities that will stimulate a child's natural curiosity. They also provide great activities for indoor play during even the longest stretches of bad weather! All three books show you how to save money by making your own paints, play dough, craft clays, glue, paste, and other arts-and-crafts supplies.

Toddler's Busy Book

Preschooler's Busy Book

Children's Busy Book

✦ Preschooler Play & Learn
Child-development expert Penny
Warner offers 150 ideas for games
and activities that will provide hours
of developmental learning opportunities, including bulleted lists of skills
that your preschooler is learning,
step-by-step instructions for each
game and activity, and illustrations
demonstrating how to play many of
the games.

✦ Practical Parenting Tips
The number-one selling collection of
helpful hints for parents with babies
and small children, containing 1,001
parent-tested tips for dealing with
diaper rash, nighttime crying, toilet
training, temper tantrums, traveling
with tots, and lots more. Parents will
save time, trouble, and money.

✦ Healthy Food for Healthy Kids
A practical guide to selecting and
preparing healthy meals for kids and
teaching healthy attitudes toward
food. More than just a cookbook, this
is a user-friendly book with real-
world advice for parents who want
their children to eat better.

✦ *When You Were a Baby*

This one-of-a-kind baby record book is designed with a die-cut hole that enables parents to prominently feature baby's photograph on every page. Baby's photo will be featured in illustrations showing crawling, first bath, first word, and more.

✦ *When You Were One*

Following the tremendous success of *When You Were a Baby,* Amanda Haley introduces the second book in her delightful record book series.

Now parents can record their child's second year in this beautifully illustrated keepsake.

✦ *When I Grow Up*

This is a book that you "write" with your child. Record his or her thoughts on future careers. A die-cut hole prominently features your child's photo on every page.

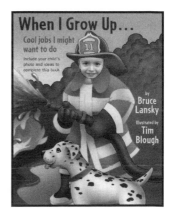

Also from Meadowbrook Press

✦ **Feed Me I'm Yours**
Parents love this easy-to-use, economical guide to making baby and toddler food at home. More than 200 recipes cover everything a parent needs to know about teething foods, nutritious snacks, and quick, pleasing lunches.

✦ **Parent-Tested Ways to Grow Your Child's Confidence**
With 150 tested ideas designed to enhance your child's self-confidence, you'll discover great ways to share enjoyable moments together, teach important skills, celebrate special occasions, encourage creativity, and recognize achievements.

✦ **What Do You Know about Manners?**
A book about manners that kids will enjoy reading? Absolutely—and parents will love it, too! Filled with fun, imaginative ways to fine-tune a child's manners, presented in a humorous format with over 100 quiz items and illustrations.

✦ **How to Read Your Child Like a Book**
This book helps parents interpret their child's behavior by teaching parents what their child is thinking. Dr. Lynn Weiss, a nationally recognized expert on child development, explains 50 different behaviors of children from birth to age 6. You will gain new insight into such behaviors as boundary testing, irritability, selfishness, and temper tantrums.

**We offer many more titles written to delight, inform, and entertain.
To order books with a credit card or browse our full
selection of titles, visit our web site at:**

www.meadowbrookpress.com

or call toll-free to place an order, request a free catalog, or ask a question:

1-800-338-2232

Meadowbrook Press • 5451 Smetana Drive • Minnetonka, MN • 55343